Almond D

Delectable Recipes

Flavorful Fire Baba

Contents

INTRODUCTION

Almond Delights: 103 Delectable Recipes is a cookbook that celebrates the versatility and deliciousness of almonds. Almonds have been a staple ingredient in many cuisines throughout history and are known for their distinct flavor and health benefits. From sweet to savory, this cookbook offers a wide variety of recipes that showcase the beloved nut in all its forms.

The cookbook is perfect for anyone who loves almonds or wants to incorporate more of them into their diet. The recipes range from traditional almond-based desserts like marzipan and macarons to innovative dishes like almond crusted chicken and almond butter spaghetti. There are also recipes for breakfast, snacks, main courses, and even drinks.

The author, a seasoned cook and food writer, has carefully curated the recipes in this cookbook to provide a balance of flavors, textures, and nutritional value. Each recipe is accompanied by a beautiful photograph that showcases the dish and makes it easy to envision what the finished product looks like.

The introduction to the cookbook provides insights into the history and origins of almonds, as well as their nutritional benefits. Almonds are packed with vitamins, minerals, and healthy fats that make them a great addition to any diet. They are also a good source of protein, fiber, and antioxidants that help to support overall health and well-being.

The cookbook is divided into chapters according to the type of recipe, making it easy to find the perfect dish for any occasion. The first chapter, Sweet Delights, features recipes for classic almond-based desserts like almond croissants, almond marshmallows, and almond tartlets. These recipes are perfect for special occasions or for when you want to indulge in a sweet treat.

The second chapter, Savory Delights, showcases recipes for appetizers, entrees, and side dishes that use almonds in creative and unexpected ways. Some of the standout recipes in this chapter include almond and goat cheese stuffed mushrooms, garlic roasted almonds, and almond crusted pork chops.

The third chapter, Breakfast and Brunch, includes recipes for almond-based breakfast dishes like almond pancakes, almond granola, and almond milk chia pudding. These dishes are great for starting the day on a healthy and delicious note.

The fourth chapter, Snacks and Nibbles, features recipes for quick and easy snacks that are perfect for busy days or for entertaining guests. Some of the recipes in this chapter include almond butter and apple slices, almond and rosemary popcorn, and almond and honey energy bites.

The fifth chapter, Main Courses, includes recipes for hearty dishes that use almonds as a primary ingredient. Some of the standout recipes in this chapter include almond crusted chicken, almond crusted fish, and almond and vegetable stir fry.

The sixth and final chapter, Drinks, showcases recipes for almond-based drinks like almond milk lattes, almond smoothies, and almond hot chocolate. These recipes are perfect for when you want to enjoy the taste and health benefits of almonds in liquid form.

Overall, Almond Delights: 103 Delectable Recipes is a must-have cookbook for anyone who loves almonds or wants to incorporate more of them into their diet. With its wide variety of recipes, beautiful photographs, and insightful introduction, this cookbook is sure to become a favorite in any kitchen.

1. Almond-crusted chicken

Almond-crusted Chicken
Serving: 4
Preparation Time: 10 minutes
Ready Time: 25 minutes

Ingredients:
• 4 boneless, skinless chicken breasts
• 1/2 cup flour
• 1 teaspoon garlic powder
• 2 eggs, beaten
• 1/2 cup almond meal
• 2 tablespoons olive oil
• 2 tablespoons vegetable oil
• Salt and pepper

Instructions:
1. Preheat oven to 375°F.
2. Place chicken breasts in a shallow bowl and season with salt and pepper
3. In a separate shallow bowl, mix together flour and garlic powder.
4. In another shallow bowl, place egg.
5. In a fourth shallow bowl, mix almond meal with olive oil.
6. Dip chicken breasts into the flour mixture, lightly coat both sides.
7. Dip in egg mixture, and then into almond meal mixture, pressing to adhere.
8. Heat olive and vegetable oil in a large skillet over medium high heat.
9. Place chicken breasts in the skillet and cook until lightly browned, about 4-5 minutes per side.
10. Place chicken breasts on a baking sheet and bake in preheated oven for 20 minutes, until cooked through and no longer pink inside.

Nutrition Information (per serving):
• Calories: 362
• Total Fat: 20 g
• Cholesterol: 90 mg
• Sodium: 153 mg

- Potassium: 269 mg
- Total Carbohydrates: 13.1 g
- Dietary Fiber: 1.7 g
- Protein: 25.3 g

2. Almond-crusted fish

Almond-crusted Fish: This almond-crusted fish dish is a flavorful and simple way to enjoy fresh, white fish. It is savory and crunchy yet light and flaky - perfect for a week night meal or a special occasion.
Serving: 8
Preparation Time: 20 minutes
Ready Time: 40 minutes

Ingredients:
- 2 lbs of white fish fillets
- 2 cups of ground almonds
- 3/4 cup bread crumbs
- 1 teaspoon of cumin
- 1/2 teaspoon of turmeric
- 1/2 teaspoon of garlic powder
- 1/4 teaspoon of paprika
- 2 tablespoons of olive oil
- 2 eggs
- Salt and pepper to taste

Instructions:
1. Preheat oven to 400 degrees Fahrenheit.
2. In a shallow bowl, beat eggs lightly. In another shallow bowl, mix together the ground almonds, bread crumbs, cumin, turmeric, garlic powder, and paprika.
3. Dip each piece of fish into the egg, coating both sides. Then, press the fish into the almond mixture, making sure it is completely coated.
4. Place the fish onto a greased baking sheet. Drizzle olive oil over each piece of fish.
5. Bake for 20 minutes or until the fish is fully cooked.

Nutrition Information:

Serving Size: 4 oz (112g)
Calories: 220
Fat: 11g
Carbohydrates: 10g
Protein: 20g
Sodium: 210mg
Cholesterol: 55mg

3. Almond butter

Almond butter is a delicious nut butter that's rich in protein and healthy fats. It's an ideal substitute for peanut butter or a wonderful addition to smoothies, toast, or other recipes.
Serving: 4 servings
Preparation Time: 10 minutes
Ready Time: 10 minutes

Ingredients:
- 2 cups of raw almonds
- Pinch of salt (optional)
- 1 teaspoon of cinnamon (optional)

Instructions:
1. Preheat oven to 350°F (177°C) and spread almonds on a baking sheet. Roast for 8-12 minutes or until golden brown.
2. Once almonds have cooled, add them to a food processor and blend until a paste forms. This should take about 5 minutes.
3. Once almonds are blended, add a pinch of salt and cinnamon (optional). Pulse the mixture for an additional 3 minutes.
4. Store the Almond Butter in an airtight container and keep in the refrigerator for up to 2 weeks.

Nutrition Information: Per serving (2 tablespoons): 176 calories, 15.2g fat, 5.5g carbohydrates, 6.3g protein, 1.6g fiber.

4. Almond milk

Deliciously creamy Almond milk is made simply by blending body-nourishing almonds with water. Almond milk is a great dairy-free alternative to regular milk and can be used in virtually any recipe that calls for milk or cream.

Serving: Makes 2-3 cups
Preparation Time: 15 minutes
Ready Time: 15 minutes

Ingredients:
1 cup raw almonds
3 cups cold filtered water
Pinch of Sea Salt (optional)

Instructions:
1. Soak almonds in a medium bowl filled with filtered water for at least 4 hours, or ideally overnight.
2. Drain and rinse almonds with fresh water.
3. Place almonds, 3 cups of cold filtered water, and a pinch of sea salt (optional, but adds flavor) in a high-powered blender, and blend on high for about 1-2 minutes, or until smooth and creamy.
4. Strain the almond milk through a cheesecloth, nut milk bag, or fine mesh sieve to remove the almond pulp.
5. Gently squeeze the excess liquid from the almond pulp, and reserve the liquid for a future recipe, such as Almond Flour Tortillas.
6. Store almond milk in a sealed container in the refrigerator, and enjoy within 4-5 days.

Nutrition Information: Almond milk is a good source of vitamin B-12, zinc, and vitamin E. It also contains calcium and magnesium, essential for strong bones and healthy muscle function. Each cup of almond milk provides approximately 70-90 calories.

5. Almond flour pancakes

These almond flour pancakes are a wonderfully tasty and healthy alternative to the traditional pancakes. They are naturally gluten-free and are filled with healthy fats and protein!
Serving:

Makes 8 pancakes
Preparation Time: 10 minutes
Ready Time: 10 minutes

Ingredients:
-1 ½ cup of almond flour
-2 tablespoons of melted coconut oil
-1 teaspoon of baking soda
-1 teaspoon of salt
-1 teaspoon of maple syrup
-3 eggs
-1 teaspoon of vanilla
-2 tablespoons of almond butter

Instructions:
1. In a medium-sized bowl, mix together almond flour, baking soda, and salt.
2. In another bowl, whisk together eggs, coconut oil, maple syrup, and vanilla.
3. Gently fold wet Ingredients into dry Ingredients until the batter is combined.
4. Heat a non-stick skillet and coat with cooking spray.
5. Using a ¼ cup scoop, spoon pancakes onto the skillet and cook for 2-3 minutes each side or until golden.
6. Serve with almond butter or other desired toppings.

Nutrition Information:
Serving Size: 1 pancake
Calories: 154
Fat: 12 g
Carbohydrates: 5 g
Protein: 4 g
Sugar: 1 g

6. Almond flour muffins

Almond Flour Muffins
Serving: 12 muffins

Preparation Time: 10 minutes
Ready Time: 25 minutes

Ingredients:
- 1/2 cup butter, melted
- 2 large eggs
- 1/2 cup coconut sugar
- 2 teaspoons pure almond extract
- 2 1/2 cups blanched almond flour
- 1 teaspoon baking soda
- 1 teaspoon ground cinnamon
- 1/4 teaspoon sea salt

Instructions:
1. Preheat your oven to 350°F. Prepare a 12-cup muffin tin with liners.
2. In a small bowl, whisk together the melted butter, eggs, coconut sugar and almond extract until smooth.
3. In a large bowl, stir together the almond flour, baking soda, cinnamon and salt.
4. Pour the wet Ingredients into the dry Ingredients and whisk until incorporated.
5. Divide the batter evenly between the muffin liners, filling them 3/4 of the way full.
6. Bake the muffins in preheated oven for 20 to 25 minutes, or until golden brown.
7. Cool for 5 minutes in the tins before transferring to a wire cooling rack.

Nutrition Information:
Each muffin contains approximately 201 calories, 16.4g fat, 11.9g carbohydrates, 5.1g protein, and 3.1g fiber.

7. Almond flour bread

Almond Flour Bread – a simple, gluten-free bread recipe perfect for breakfast or snacking.
Serving: 6 servings
Preparation Time: 10 minutes

Ready Time: 60 minutes

Ingredients:
- 3 ½ cups almond flour
- 6 large eggs
- 3 tablespoons olive oil
- 2 teaspoons sea salt
- 1 tablespoon baking soda

Instructions:
1. Preheat oven to 350 degrees F (176°C).
2. In a medium bowl, mix together almond flour, sea salt, and baking soda.
3. In a separate large bowl, whisk together eggs and olive oil.
4. Slowly, add wet Ingredients to the dry Ingredients, mixing together until fully combined.
5. Grease a 9x5-inch loaf pan with oil or butter.
6. Pour the almond flour batter into the loaf pan and spread evenly.
7. Bake for 40-50 minutes, or until a toothpick inserted into the center comes out clean.
8. Cool for 10 minutes before slicing and serving.

Nutrition Information:
Per Serving: 259 calories, 8.2 g protein, 25.5 g fat, 7.7 g carbohydrates, 3.9 g sugar, 4.7 g fiber, 719 mg sodium

8. Almond flour waffles

Almond flour waffles are delicious waffles made with gluten-free almond flour, giving them a delightfully light and fluffy texture.
Serving: 6 waffles
Preparation Time: 10 minutes
Ready Time: 10-15 minutes

Ingredients:
1½ cups almond flour
½ teaspoon baking soda
¼ teaspoon salt

2 teaspoons pure maple syrup
4 eggs
2 tablespoons melted butter

Instructions:
1. Preheat a waffle iron.
2. In a mixing bowl, whisk together the almond flour, baking soda, and salt.
3. In a separate bowl, whisk together the maple syrup, eggs, and melted butter.
4. Pour the wet Ingredients into the dry Ingredients and stir until combined.
5. Grease the preheated waffle iron and spoon 1/4 cup of the batter into each section of the iron.
6. Close the iron and cook for 4-5 minutes or until waffles are golden and slightly crispy.
7. Serve with your favorite toppings.

Nutrition Information: Serving Size: 1 waffle (1/6 of recipe), Calories: 180, Fat: 12g, Carbohydrates: 7g, Protein: 11g.

9. Almond flour cookies

Almond Flour Cookies
Serving: Makes about 12 cookies
Preparation Time: 10 min
Ready Time: 20 min

Ingredients:
- 1/2 cup butter, softened
- 1/2 cup granulated sugar
- 1/2 cup almond flour
- 1/4 teaspoon baking powder
- 1/2 teaspoon vanilla extract
- 1 large egg

Instructions:
1. Preheat oven to 350°F. Line a baking sheet with parchment paper.

2. In a large bowl, combine butter and sugar using a hand mixer. Beat until creamy.
3. In a separate bowl, whisk together the almond flour and baking powder.
4. Add the almond flour mixture to the butter mixture and mix until combined.
5. Add the vanilla extract and egg and mix until fully incorporated.
6. Using a spoon, drop batter onto the lined baking sheet, about 2 inches apart.
7. Bake for 15-20 minutes, or until lightly golden brown on the edges.
8. Cool on a wire rack and enjoy!

Nutrition Information (Per Cookie):
Calories: 91 kcal | Carbohydrates: 5.6 g | Protein: 1.8 g | Fat: 6.5 g | Sugar: 4.2 g

10. Almond flour pie crust

Almond flour pie crust
Serving: 6
Preparation time: 10 minutes
Ready time: 25 minutes

Ingredients:
1 cup almond flour
3 tablespoons coconut sugar
½ teaspoon sea salt
3 tablespoons coconut oil, melted

Instructions:
1. Preheat oven to 350°F/175°C.
2. In a medium bowl, mix together almond flour, coconut sugar, and sea salt.
3. Add melted coconut oil and mix until well combined and a crumbly texture is achieved.
4. Press the dough firmly into an 8-inch pie dish.
5. Bake for 15 minutes or until the crust is golden brown.

Nutrition Information:
Serving size: 1/6 of pie crust
Calories: 170
Fat: 12g
Carbohydrates: 12g
Protein: 3g
Fiber: 3g

11. Almond flour pizza crust

Almond Flour Pizza Crust - A delicious pizza crust made with almond flour for a nutritious low-carb alternative to traditional pizza.
Serving: Makes one 9-inch pizza crust.
Preparation time: 10 minutes
Ready time: 25 minutes

Ingredients:
-1 cup almond flour
-2 tablespoons flaxseed meal
-½ teaspoon sea salt
-½ teaspoon garlic powder
-2 tablespoons olive oil
-4 tablespoons water

Instructions:
1. Preheat oven to 375°F.
2. In a medium bowl, combine almond flour, flaxseed meal, sea salt, and garlic powder.
3. Add olive oil and water and mix together to form a sticky dough.
4. Press dough into a greased 9-inch cake pan, making sure to press it evenly up the sides.
5. Bake for 20-25 minutes or until golden.
6. Remove from oven and let cool for 10 minutes before adding toppings.
7. Place back in the oven and bake for an additional 10 minutes or until cheese is melted and toppings are cooked to your preference.

Nutrition Information:

Calories: 263, Fat: 13 g (Saturated 1 g, Polyunsaturated 0 g, Monounsaturated 11 g), Cholesterol: 0 mg, Sodium: 401 mg, Potassium: 13 mg, Carbohydrates: 19 g (Fiber 5 g, Sugar 2 g), Protein: 13 g.

12. Almond flour crackers

Almond flour crackers are an easy and healthy snack that the whole family can enjoy! This crispy-crunchy snack is gluten-free, dairy-free, and full of protein and fiber.
Serving: Makes about 25-30 crackers
Preparation Time: 10 minutes
Ready Time: 25 minutes

Ingredients:
-1 cup almond flour
-2 tablespoons cold butter
-2 tablespoons grated parmesan cheese
-2 tablespoons sesame seeds
-¼ teaspoon garlic powder
-¼ teaspoon salt
-2 tablespoons cold water

Instructions:
1. Preheat oven to 350°F. Line a baking sheet with parchment paper and set aside.
2. In a medium bowl, mix together almond flour, butter, cheese, sesame seeds, garlic powder, and salt until crumbly.
3. Add in water and mix until dough comes together.
4. Using your hands, roll dough into a log, about 12 inches long. Cut into 1/4-inch slices.
5. Place slices on baking sheet and bake for 25 minutes, until lightly golden.
6. Allow to cool before serving.

Nutrition Information (per serving):
Calories: 70
Total Fat: 5.4g
Saturated Fat: 1.5g

Cholesterol: 6mg
Sodium: 72mg
Carbohydrates: 3g
Fiber: 0.7g
Sugar: 0.2g
Protein: 2.4g

13. Almond milk smoothies

Almond milk smoothies
Serving: 2
Preparation Time: 5 minutes
Ready Time: 5 minutes

Ingredients:
1/2 cup rolled oats
2 tablespoons ground almonds
1/4 teaspoon ground cinnamon
1 banana
1/2 cup almond milk
1/4 cup crushed ice

Instructions:
1. Place the oats, almonds, and cinnamon in a blender and mix until they are combined and a flour-like consistency is formed.
2. Add the banana and almond milk and blend until a thick, smooth mixture is formed.
3. Add crushed ice and blend again until the smoothie is thick and creamy.

Nutrition Information:
Calories: 140, Total Fat: 5g, Saturated Fat: 0g, Cholesterol 0mg, Sodium 25mg, Total Carbohydrate: 20.6g, Dietary Fiber: 2.9g, Sugars: 6.6g, Protein: 4g

14. Almond milk hot chocolate

Almond milk hot chocolate is a creamy and delicious beverage that's also vegan-friendly. It's the perfect choice for a cozy winter night or even a movie night with friends. Serve it up with whipped cream, extra chocolate, and a few marshmallows for an extra special treat.
Serving: 6
Preparation Time: 5 minutes
Ready Time: 10 minutes

Ingredients:
- 2 cups almond milk
- 6 tablespoons cocoa powder
- 3 tablespoons maple syrup
- 2 tablespoons sugar
- Pinch of sea salt
- ½ teaspoon vanilla extract

Instructions:
1. Heat the almond milk in a small saucepan over medium high heat.
2. Once hot, whisk in cocoa powder, maple syrup, sugar, sea salt, and vanilla.
3. Continue to whisk until the mixture is well combined and heats through.
4. Pour the hot chocolate into mugs and enjoy.

Nutrition Information: 92 calories per serving, 4 g fat, 16 g carbohydrates, 2 g protein.

15. Almond milk ice cream

Almond Milk Ice Cream is an incredibly creamy, richly indulgent frozen dessert made with almond milk. It's the perfect vegan ice cream for a sweet and creamy summer treat!
Serving: 4 servings
Preparation Time: 10 minutes
Ready Time: 8 hours

Ingredients:
- 2 cups almond milk

- 2/3 cup granulated sugar
- 1/8 teaspoon salt
- 1 teaspoon almond extract
- 1 tablespoon cornstarch

Instructions:
1. In a medium saucepan, combine the almond milk, sugar, and salt. Cook over medium heat and stir occasionally until the sugar dissolves.
2. In a small bowl, mix together the almond extract and cornstarch until blended.
3. Add the almond extract and cornstarch mixture to the saucepan and stir until combined. Continue to heat until the mixture comes to a low boil.
4. Remove the pan from the heat and strain the mixture into a heat-proof bowl. Allow to cool.
5. Once cooled, transfer the mixture to an ice cream maker and churn for about 20 minutes, or according to manufacturer's Instructions.
6. Transfer the ice cream to an air tight container and place in the freezer for at least 8 hours before serving.

Nutrition Information:
Serving size: 1/4 cup (50g)
Calories: 97kcal, Fat: 0.7g, Carbohydrates: 20.9g, Protein: 1.6g

16. Almond oil vinaigrette

Made with just a few simple Ingredients, this Almond Oil Vinaigrette is an easy and delicious option for any salad.
Serving: 4
Preparation Time: 10 minutes
Ready Time: 10 minutes

Ingredients:
- 2 tbsp almond oil
- 2 garlic cloves, minced
- 2 tbsp white balsamic vinegar
- 2 tsp Dijon mustard
- 1/4 tsp fine sea salt

- Freshly ground black pepper

Instructions:
1. In a small bowl, whisk together almond oil, garlic, vinegar, mustard, salt and pepper.
2. Taste and adjust Ingredients according to preference.
3. Whisk again before serving.

Nutrition Information (based on ¼ cup): 140 calories; 14g fat; 0.4g carbohydrates; 0.04g protein.

17. Almond oil mayonnaise

Almond oil mayonnaise is a healthy alternative to traditional mayonnaise, packed with flavor and essential healthy fats. Not only is it delicious, but it's incredibly simple to make, taking just minutes to prepare. With almond oil as the base to provide lots of health benefits, you can feel good about enjoying this mayonnaise.
Serving
Makes 1 cup of mayonnaise.
Preparation Time
5 minutes
Ready Time
5 minutes

Ingredients:
- 1 large egg
- 1 Tbsp freshly squeezed lemon juice
- 1/2 tsp Dijon mustard
- 3/4 cup almond oil
- 1/4 tsp sea salt
- 1/4 tsp ground black pepper

Instructions:
1. In a medium bowl, whisk together the egg, lemon juice, and mustard until well blended.
2. Slowly add in the almond oil, one tablespoon at a time, while whisking to combine.

3. Once all of the oil is incorporated, whisk in the salt and pepper.
4. Taste and adjust seasoning if needed.

Nutrition Information
Serving size: 1 Tbsp
Calories: 94
Total Fat: 10.4 g
Saturated Fat: 0.6 g
Cholesterol: 8.2 mg
Sodium: 16.9 mg
Total Carbohydrates: 0.2 g
Protein: 0.5 g

18. Chocolate-covered almonds

Chocolate-covered almonds
Serving: 10
Preparation time: 10 minutes
Ready time: 30 minutes

Ingredients:
- 200g whole almonds, blanched
- 150g semi-sweet or dark chocolate chips
- 2 teaspoons coconut oil

Instructions:
1. Preheat oven to 350°F (175°C) and spread almonds out in a shallow baking pan.
2. Roast almonds in the preheated oven for 7 to 10 minutes, stirring them around in the pan halfway through.
3. Remove from the oven and let cool.
4. Melt chocolate chips along with the coconut oil in a microwave in 30-second intervals, stirring between each interval.
3. Once the chocolate is melted, add in the almonds and stir to coat.
4. Line a plate or a cookie sheet with parchment paper and spread the almonds out onto it.
5. Let the chocolate harden completely before transferring the almonds to an airtight container for storage.

Nutrition Information (per serving):
Calories: 204
Total Fat: 14.9 g
Saturated Fat: 6.1 g
Carbohydrates: 13.4 g
Protein: 5.9 g
Fiber: 2.5 g
Sodium: 1.6 mg

19. Spiced almonds

Spiced Almonds
Serving: 4
Preparation Time: 5 minutes
Ready Time: 10 minutes

Ingredients:
• 1 cup raw almonds
• 2 tablespoons olive oil
• ¼ teaspoon garlic powder
• ½ teaspoon paprika
• ½ teaspoon Italian seasoning
• ¼ teaspoon of sea/kosher salt

Instructions:
1. Preheat oven to 375 degrees.
2. In a bowl, combine the almonds, olive oil, garlic powder, paprika, Italian seasoning, and salt. Mix until the almonds are evenly coated.
3. Place the coated almonds onto a parchment-lined baking sheet.
4. Bake for 10 minutes.
5. Remove from the oven and cool before serving.

Nutrition Information:
Serving size: ¼ cup
Calories: 213
Fat: 16.7 g
Carbohydrates: 3.7 g

Fiber: 2.3 g

20. Almond biscotti

Almond biscotti is a classic Italian cookie that is known for its crunchy texture and lightly sweet flavor. Enjoy it with tea, coffee, or as an afternoon snack.
Serving: Makes approximately 16 biscotti
Preparation Time: 10 minutes
Ready Time: 40 minutes

Ingredients:
2 cups all-purpose flour
1 teaspoon baking powder
1/4 teaspoon salt
3 large eggs
1 cup sugar
1 teaspoon almond extract
3/4 cup almonds, chopped

Instructions:
1. Preheat oven to 350°F and line a baking sheet with parchment paper or a silicone mat.
2. In a medium bowl, stir together the flour, baking powder and salt.
3. In a large bowl, whisk together the eggs, sugar and almond extract until light and foamy.
4. Gradually add the dry Ingredients to the egg mixture and mix until a stiff dough forms. Fold in the chopped almonds.
5. Divide the dough into two equal sections. Use wet hands or a rolling pin to flatten each section into a log shape about 1-inch thick.
6. Place the logs onto the prepared baking sheet, and bake for 20-25 minutes, or until golden brown.
7. Allow to cool for 10 minutes. Reduce the oven temperature to 325°F.
8. Cut the logs into 1/2-inch slices and arrange on the baking sheet. Bake for 10-15 minutes more, or until lightly toasted.
9. Allow the biscotti to cool completely before serving.

Nutrition Information: Serving size: 1 biscotti; Calories: 80; Fat: 3g; Carbs: 11g; Protein: 3g; Sodium: 25mg; Sugar: 5g

21. Almond macarons

Almond Macarons
Serving: 20-24 macarons
Preparation time: 2 hrs
Ready time: 3 hrs

Ingredients:
• 3 large egg whites
• ¾ cup/148g superfine sugar
• 2½ cups/212 g almond meal
• ¼ cup/36g icing sugar
• 2 - 5 drops almond extract

Instructions:
1. Create a meringue by beating the egg whites and superfine sugar until stiff peaks are formed.
2. Combine almond meal and icing sugar in a separate bowl.
3. Sift the almond meal and icing sugar mixture through a sieve into the meringue and fold gently until combined. Add the almond extract to combine.
4. Fill a piping bag with the mixture and pipe onto a parchment-lined baking tray.
5. Tap the baking trays lightly on the counter to release any air bubbles.
6. Allow the macarons to sit for at least 30 minutes to form a skin.
7. Preheat oven to 300°F/150°C.
8. Bake for 15-17 minutes. Allow to cool completely.
9. Assemble the macarons with almond buttercream or any other filling of your choice.

Nutrition Information:
Calories: 67 kcal, Carbohydrates: 10 g, Protein: 1.8 g, Fat: 2.4 g, Saturated Fat: 0.3 g, Cholesterol: 0 mg, Sodium: 1 mg, Potassium: 20 mg, Fiber: 1.1 g, Sugar: 8.2 g, Vitamin A: 0.6%, Vitamin C: 0%, Calcium: 2.2%, Iron: 2.4%

22. Almond croissants

Almond Croissants are a delicious and indulgent breakfast or snack made with croissant dough, almond paste, and flaked almonds. This festive treat is a unique and flavorful spin on a traditional breakfast pastry.
Serving: 8
Preparation Time: 25 minutes
Ready Time: 55 minutes

Ingredients:
- 2 boxes puff pastry croissants
- 2/3 cup almond paste, cut into 8 pieces
- 2/3 cup flaked almonds
- Powdered sugar, for garnish

Instructions:
1. Preheat oven to 375°F.
2. Unroll puff pastry onto a lightly floured surface and cut into 8 rectangles.
3. Place a piece of almond paste in the center of 4 of the rectangles.
4. Top with the remaining puff pastry rectangles and seal the edges.
5. Cut slits into the top of the croissants and sprinkle with flaked almonds.
6. Bake for 25-30 minutes, or until golden brown.
7. Let cool before serving and dust with powdered sugar, if desired.

Nutrition Information: Per serving: 334 calories, 17.9g total fat, 8.3g saturated fat, 181mg sodium, 37.8g carbs, 3.2g fiber, 4.5g sugar, and 6g protein.

23. Almond Danish

Almond Danish
Serving: 8
Preparation Time: 10 minutes
Ready Time: 25 minutes

Ingredients:
- 2 ½ cups all-purpose flour
- 2 teaspoons baking powder
- ¼ teaspoon salt
- ½ cup (1 stick) butter, at room temperature
- ½ cup granulated sugar
- 1 teaspoon almond extract
- 2 large eggs
- ¼ cup heavy cream
- ¾ cup sliced almonds
- White glaze, if desired

Instructions:
1. Preheat oven to 375°F. Grease a 9x13-inch baking pan with butter and set aside.
2. In a medium bowl, whisk together flour, baking powder, and salt to combine. Set aside.
3. In the bowl of a stand mixer or using a hand mixer, beat the butter and sugar until light and fluffy, about 3 minutes. Beat in almond extract and eggs, one at a time, until combined.
4. Gradually add in the dry Ingredients to the butter mixture, mixing until just combined. Stir in the cream and almonds.
5. Spread the batter into the prepared pan. Bake for 20-25 minutes, or until golden brown. Allow to cool completely before drizzling with white glaze, if desired. Cut into 8 pieces to serve.

Nutrition Information: (serving size of 1 piece):
Calories: 250
Fat: 14g
Carbohydrates: 25g
Protein: 5g
Sodium: 94mg

24. Almond cappuccino

Almond Cappuccino is a delicious coffee-based drink with almond syrup and steamed milk! This creamy and smooth beverage can be easily made at home with a few Ingredients and a few simple steps.

Serving: 1
Preparation Time: 5 minutes
Ready Time: 5 minutes

Ingredients:
- 2 shots of espresso
- 2 tablespoons almond syrup
- 2 tablespoons granulated sugar
- ½ cup whole milk
- Whipped cream (optional)

Instructions:
1. Prepare two shots of espresso according to your machine's Instructions.
2. In a small microwave-safe cup, add almond syrup and granulated sugar. Put the cup in the oven and heat for 30 seconds.
3. In a tall drinking glass, add the heated almond syrup and espresso shots.
4. Put the milk in a milk frother and steam until it has doubled in size.
5. Pour the steamed milk into the glass with the espresso shots and syrup. Stir with a spoon to combine.
6. Top with a dollop of whipped cream (optional).

Nutrition Information:
Calories: 155;
Fat: 6 g;
Carbohydrates: 16 g;
Protein: 7 g.

25. Almond latte

Almond Latte
Looking for a non-dairy latte option? Look no further than this creamy almond latte recipe! Made with almond milk and almond extract, this

latte is the perfect way to enjoy the comforting taste of your favorite coffee shop drink, without any of the dairy.
Serving: 1 latte
Preparation time: 5 minutes
Ready time: 5 minutes

Ingredients:
- 1 cup unsweetened almond milk
- 1 shot of espresso
- 1/4 tsp almond extract
- 1 tsp sweetener of your choice (optional)

Instructions:
1. In a saucepan over medium heat, warm the almond milk until it is steaming but not boiling.
2. Meanwhile, brew a shot of espresso in a mug.
3. Add the almond extract and optional sweetener to the almond milk, and whisk until frothy.
4. Pour the almond milk mixture over the espresso.
5. Use a spoon to hold back the foam as you pour, then top with the remaining foam.

Nutrition Information:
Calories - 70
Total Fat - 4g
Saturated Fat - 0g
Cholesterol - 0mg
Sodium - 110mg
Total Carbohydrate - 6g
Dietary Fiber - 1g
Total Sugars - 2g
Protein - 2g

26. Almond chai tea

Almond Chai Tea
Serving: 2
Preparation Time: 5 minutes

Ready Time: 10 minutes

Ingredients:
- 2 cups of water
- 2 teaspoons of black tea leaves
- 1 teaspoon of almond extract
- 2 three-inch cinnamon sticks
- 2 tablespoons of honey
- Milk (optional)

Instructions:
1. Bring the two cups of water to a boil in a small pot.
2. Add the tea leaves, almond extract, and cinnamon sticks and stir. Let the mixture come to boil for one minute.
3. Turn off the heat, cover the pot, and let it steep for at least five minutes.
4. Remove the cinnamon sticks and add the honey to the tea and stir until dissolved.
5. Pour the chai tea into two mugs.
6. Optionally, add some milk to each mug before serving.

Nutrition Information:
Serving Size: 2 cups, Calories: 63, Total Fat: 0g, Sodium: 10.3mg, Potassium: 49.2mg, Total Carbohydrates: 16.1g, Sugars: 9.9g, Protein: 0.7g.

27. Almond brittle

Almond brittle is a delicious snack that is perfect for enjoying with a cup of tea or coffee.
Serving: Makes 12 servings
Preparation Time: 10 minutes
Ready Time: 60 minutes

Ingredients:
- 2 cups white sugar
- 1 cup water
- ¼ teaspoon baking soda

- ¼ teaspoon salt
- ¼ teaspoon vanilla extract
- 1 ½ cups whole almonds

Instructions:
1. Grease a large baking sheet with butter.
2. In a large pot, combine the sugar, water, baking soda, and salt. Cook over medium-high heat, stirring constantly, until the mixture reaches 310°F on a candy thermometer.
3. Remove from heat and stir in the vanilla extract and almonds.
4. Pour the mixture onto the prepared baking sheet and spread it into a thin, even layer. Allow to cool completely.
5. Break the almond brittle into pieces and enjoy!

Nutrition Information: Per Serving: 312 calories, 58.5 g carbohydrates, 2.2 g protein, 11.6 g fat.

28. Almond bark

Almond Bark is a deliciously unique combination of crunchy almonds and smooth chocolate. It's the perfect snack or addition to any dessert!
Serving: 10 - 12
Preparation Time: 15 minutes
Ready Time: 30 minutes

Ingredients:
- 12 ounces semi-sweet chocolate chips
- 2 cups sliced, toasted almonds
- 1 tablespoon coconut oil

Instructions:
1. Preheat oven to 350° F. Spread almonds onto a baking sheet and toast for 5-7 minutes until lightly browned.
2. Melt chocolate chips in a microwave-safe bowl, stirring at intervals until smooth.
3. Add the melted chocolate, toasted almonds, and coconut oil to a medium-sized bowl and stir until combined.

4. Line a baking sheet with parchment paper, then pour and spread the almond bark mixture onto the parchment paper.
5. Place the almond bark in the refrigerator for 15-20 minutes to cool.
6. Break the almond bark into desired sizes and enjoy!

Nutrition Information:
Serving size: 1 piece
Calories: 105
Total Fat: 6g
Saturated Fat: 2.5g
Carbohydrates: 11g
Sugar: 8g
Protein: 2.5g

29. Almond nougat

Almond nougat is a delicious sweet treat to enjoy featuring chewy nougat, crunchy almonds, and rich vanilla.
Serving: 4
Preparation Time: 1 hour
Ready Time: 1 hour 10 minutes

Ingredients:
- 100g sugar
- 75g honey
- 75g butter
- 75g grated almonds
- 15ml vanilla extract
- 2 sheets edible rice paper

Instructions:
1. Preheat the oven to 160C (320F).
2. Line a baking tray with greaseproof paper.
3. In a small saucepan, mix together the sugar, honey and butter.
4. Heat on low heat, stirring occasionally until all the Ingredients are combined and melted.
5. Take off the heat and stir in the almonds and vanilla extract.
6. Spread the mixture on to the baking tray, and flatten with a spatula.

7. Place in the preheated oven and bake for around 20 minutes or until the top is golden brown and the nougat is bubbling.
8. Place the two sheets of edible rice paper on top of each other and use the rolling pin to lightly flatten the nougat sandwiching the two sheets together.
9. Cut into desired shapes and leave to cool before serving.

Nutrition Information:
Each serving of almond nougat contains approximately 250 calories, 15g fat, 31g carbohydrates, 1g protein, and 86mg sodium.

30. Almond cake

Almond Cake
Serving: 8-10
Preparation Time: 15 minutes
Ready Time: 45 minutes

Ingredients:
- 2 cups all-purpose flour
- 1 cup ground almonds
- 1/2 teaspoon baking powder
- 1 teaspoon baking soda
- 3 eggs
- 2/3 cup vegetable oil
- 1 teaspoon almond extract
- 2 cups white sugar

Instructions:
1. Preheat oven to 350 degrees F (175 degrees C). Grease and flour one 9x13 inch baking pan.
2. In a large bowl, mix together the flour, ground almonds, baking soda, and baking powder.
3. In a separate bowl, combine the eggs, oil, almond extract, and sugar.
4. Add the egg mixture to the dry Ingredients, and mix until thoroughly blended. Pour the batter into the prepared pan.
5. Bake for 40 to 45 minutes in the preheated oven. Allow to cool before serving.

Nutrition Information: about 350 calories per serving, 17 grams of fat, 52 grams of carbohydrates, 3 grams of protein.

31. Almond tarts

Decadent and full of flavor, almond tarts are a perfect dessert option for any occasion. Made with a crumbly pastry crust and a homemade almond filling, these tarts are sweet, fragrant, and simply delightful.
Serving: Makes 6 tarts
Preparation Time: 15 minutes
Ready Time: 1 hour 10 minutes

Ingredients:
For the Crust:
- 1 ¼ cups all-purpose flour
- 4 tablespoons sugar
- ¼ teaspoon salt
- ½ cup cold unsalted butter, cubed
For the Filling:
- 1 cup ground almonds
- ½ cup sugar
- 2 tablespoons all-purpose flour
- 2 tablespoons unsalted butter, melted
- 1 large egg
- ½ teaspoon almond extract

Instructions:
1. To prepare the crust: Preheat oven to 350°F. Line a 6-hole tart pan with removable bases with parchment paper.
2. In a large bowl, mix together the flour, sugar and salt. Using a pastry cutter, cut the butter into the flour mixture until the mixture forms small crumbs.
3. Divide the mixture among the tart pans, and press the mixture into the base. Prick the bases with a fork. Bake for 20 minutes or until golden brown. Allow to cool.

4. To prepare the filling: In a large bowl, mix together the ground almonds, sugar, flour, melted butter, egg and almond extract. Stir until combined.
5. Divide the mixture among the cooled tart bases. Bake for 30-35 minutes until golden brown and set. Allow to cool before serving.

Nutrition Information:
Serving Size: 1 tart
Calories: 216
Fat: 13g
Carbohydrates: 19.5g
Protein: 4.5g

32. Almond fruit bars

Almond Fruit Bars are a nutritious and delicious treat for kids and adults alike. These no-bake bars feature a chewy almond base, with an oozy layer of seasonal fruit in the middle, all topped off with a bit of crunchy cereal.
Serving: Makes around 8 bars.
Preparation time: 15 minutes
Ready time: Around 30 minutes

Ingredients:
- ½ cup dried apricots
- ½ cup diced mangoes
- 2 tablespoons brown sugar
- 2 tablespoons honey
- 2 cups almonds, sliced
- ¼ teaspoon ground cinnamon
- ¼ teaspoon ground nutmeg
- ⅛ teaspoon ground cloves
- ¾ cup crunchy cereal (for the topping)

Instructions:
1. Preheat oven to 350°F (175°C).
2. In a food processor, blend the apricots and mangoes together until smooth.

3. In a medium bowl, mix the brown sugar, honey, almonds, cinnamon, nutmeg, and cloves together.
4. Take half of the almond mix and spread it into the bottom of a lined 8 inch (20 cm) square pan.
5. Spread the fruit mixture over this and then sprinkle the remaining almond mix on top.
6. Bake for 20 minutes, until golden.
7. Take out of the oven and let cool.
8. Sprinkle the cereal on top and leave to cool down completely before slicing into bars.

Nutrition Information: One Almond Fruit Bar contains approximately 140 calories, 7g of fat, 15g of carbohydrates, 4g of fibre, and 6g of protein.

33. Almond plum cake

Almond Plum Cake is a moist and flavorful cake perfect for special occasions. It has a light almond flavor from the almond extract and is topped with fresh plums for a beautiful presentation.
Serving: 8-10
Preparation Time: 10 minutes
Ready Time: 1 hour

Ingredients:
• 2 cups all-purpose flour
• 1 teaspoon baking powder
• 1 teaspoon baking soda
• 1/4 teaspoon salt
• 1/4 teaspoon ground cinnamon
• 1/2 cup butter (softened)
• 1 cup granulated sugar
• 2 eggs
• 1 teaspoon almond extract
• 1 cup plain yogurt
• 2 cups ripe plums (diced)
• 2 tablespoons sliced almonds

Instructions:
1. Preheat oven to 350°F (175°C). Grease and flour a 9-inch round baking pan.
2. In a medium bowl, whisk together the flour, baking powder, baking soda, salt, and cinnamon.
3. In a large bowl, cream together the butter and sugar until light and fluffy. Beat in the eggs one at a time, then stir in the almond extract and yogurt.
4. Gradually stir in the dry Ingredients until fully incorporated.
5. Fold in the diced plums.
6. Spread the batter into the prepared pan and sprinkle with almonds.
7. Bake in the preheated oven for 45-50 minutes, or until a toothpick inserted into the center of the cake comes out clean.
8. Allow to cool before serving.

Nutrition Information:
Serving size: 1 slice; Calories: 224 kcal; Carbohydrates: 34 g; Fat: 8 g; Protein: 4 g; Cholesterol: 47 mg; Sodium: 160 mg; Fiber: 2 g; Sugars: 17 g.

34. Almond berry tart

Almond berry tart
Serving: 8
Preparation Time: 15 minutes
Ready Time: 55 minutes

Ingredients:
-1/2 cup almond meal
-1/4 cup whole wheat pastry flour
-1/4 teaspoon salt
-1/4 cup cold butter, cubed
-3 tablespoons cold water
-1 tablespoon cornstarch
-1/4 cup packed light brown sugar
-1/2 teaspoon cinnamon
-2 1/2 cups mixed berries
-1 tablespoon milk

-1 teaspoon sugar

Instructions:
1. Preheat oven to 375°F.
2. In a medium bowl, combine almond meal, flour and salt.
3. Using fingertips, work cubed butter into flour mixture until it resembles coarse meal.
4. Add cold water, one tablespoon at a time, and mix until the dough forms a ball.
5. Place ball of dough onto a lightly floured surface and roll into a 10-inch circle.
6. Place dough into a 9-inch tart pan and press it evenly into the sides.
7. In a small bowl, combine cornstarch, brown sugar and cinnamon; mix well.
8. Add berries and mix until berries are thoroughly coated.
9. Pour mixture into tart shell.
10. Bake for 30 minutes.
11. Brush top of tart with milk and sprinkle with sugar.
12. Bake for an additional 25 minutes or until crust is golden brown.

Nutrition Information (per serving):
Calories: 228 kcal
Fat: 15.3g
Carbohydrates: 20.5g
Protein: 3.5g
Sugar: 8.8g
Fiber: 3.5g
Sodium: 59mg

35. Almond apricot tart

Almond Apricot Tart
Serving: 8
Preparation Time: 25 minutes
Ready Time: 35 minutes

Ingredients:
-1 pre-made 9-inch tart shell

-3/4 cup almond paste
-1/4 cup whole almonds
-1/2 teaspoon ground cinnamon
-2 tablespoons butter, melted
-2/3 cup apricot jam

Instructions:
1. Preheat the oven to 350 degrees F.
2. In a medium bowl, mix together the almond paste, whole almonds, cinnamon, and melted butter until it forms a crumbly mixture.
3. Spread the apricot jam in the bottom of the tart shell.
4. Sprinkle the almond mixture over the jam, spreading it out evenly.
5. Bake in the preheated oven for 25-30 minutes, or until the edges of the tart are lightly browned and the jam is bubbling.
6. Let the tart cool for 10 minutes before slicing and serving.

Nutrition Information:
Calories: 315 kcal
Carbs: 34g
Sugar: 17g
Fat: 15g
Protein: 5g
Cholesterol: 20mg
Sodium: 140mg

36. Almond chocolate truffles

Almond Chocolate Truffles
Serving: 12
Preparation time: 20 minutes
Ready time: 1 hour

Ingredients:
- 1/3 cup of heavy whipping cream
- 6 tbsp almond butter
- 1/4 cup cocoa powder
- 2 1/2 cups semi-sweet chocolate chips
- 2 tsp almond extract

- 2 tbsp butter
- 1/2 cup toasted sliced almonds
- 2 tsp coconut oil

Instructions:
1. In a medium saucepan, heat the whipping cream, almond butter, cocoa powder, chocolate chips, almond extract and butter over medium-low heat. Stir constantly until the chocolate chips are melted and fully incorporated.
2. Pour the mixture into a bowl and set aside to cool.
3. Once cooled, roll the mixture into 1-inch balls and roll each one in the toasted almonds. Place the finished truffles onto a parchment-lined baking sheet.
4. Melt the coconut oil and lightly brush it on the top and sides of each truffle.
5. Place the baking sheet in the freezer for 1 hour.
Nutrition Facts per Truffle:
Calories: 140
Fat: 9g
Carbs: 14g
Protein: 3g

37. Almond hazelnut pralines

Almond Hazelnut Pralines are a delicious mash-up of two of the most beloved nutty flavors. These simple yet indulgent treats are quick and easy to make and great for a party or to add a bit of sweetness to your day.
Serving: 10-12 pieces
Preparation Time: 10 minutes
Ready Time: 30 minutes

Ingredients:
- 2 tablespoons ground almonds
- 3 tablespoons roasted hazelnuts, chopped
- 2/3 cup of granulated sugar
- 1/3 cup of water
- 2 tablespoons butter

- 1/4 teaspoon of almond extract

Instructions:
1. Grease a baking sheet with the butter.
2. In a saucepan, heat the sugar and water over medium-high heat until it just starts to boil. Continue to stir and cook until an amber caramel forms (about 8 minutes).
3. Reduce the heat to low and stir in the almonds, hazelnuts and almond extract.
4. Continue to stir until the mixture thickens and pulls away from the sides of the pan (about 2 minutes).
5. Remove the pan from the heat and spread the mixture over the prepared baking sheet.
6. Allow to cool for 15-20 minutes before cutting into small squares.

Nutrition Information: Each piece contains approximately 80 calories, 5g of carbohydrates, 4g of fat, and 1g of protein.

38. Almond peanut butter

Creamy and delicious almond peanut butter combines the richness of peanuts with the nutty sweetness of almonds. This easy-to-make spread is perfect for a variety of recipes and snacks.
Serving: 2 cups
Preparation Time: 15 minutes
Ready Time: 15 minutes

Ingredients:
- 2 cups of roasted salted peanuts
- 2 cups of roasted salted almonds
- ½ cup of vegetable oil
- ¼ cup of honey or agave syrup
- A pinch of sea salt

Instructions:
1. Preheat oven to 350°F (175°C).
2. Spread peanuts and almonds on a baking sheet and roast for 10 minutes.

3. Allow the peanuts and almonds to cool slightly for 5 minutes.
4. Place the peanuts and almonds into a food processor.
5. Process the peanuts and almonds until they form a coarse meal.
6. Slowly drizzle in the oil and honey while the processor is running.
7. Add pinch of salt and process until the mixture forms a smooth mixture.
8. Transfer the almond peanut butter to an airtight container.

Nutrition Information:
Serving size: 2 tablespoons
Calories: 150
Total fat: 11 g
Total Carbohydrate: 7 g
Protein: 4 g
Sodium: 35 mg

39. Almond cashew butter

Almond Cashew Butter: Almond cashew butter is a perfect blend of nuttiness and creamy texture. It is a great source of proteins and is a delicious alternative to traditional store-bought nut butters.
Serving: Makes 3/4 cup
Preparation Time: 10 minutes
Ready Time: 10 minutes

Ingredients:
-1 cup raw almonds
-1/4 cup raw cashews
-1/4 teaspoon salt
-2 teaspoons honey
-2 teaspoons coconut oil

Instructions:
1. Preheat the oven to 350 degrees Fahrenheit.
2. Spread the almonds and cashews on a baking sheet and roast in the oven for 10 minutes, stirring once or twice to ensure even roasting.
3. Once roasted, let the almonds and cashews cool for about 5 minutes before adding to a food processor.

4. Pulse the almonds and cashews in the food processor for about 20 to 30 seconds.
5. Gradually add the coconut oil, honey, and salt as you continue to process until the mixture forms a creamy butter, about 1 minute.
6. Let the almond cashew butter cool before transferring to a jar and storing in the refrigerator. Enjoy!

Nutrition Information: Per 2 tablespoon serving: Calories: 147, Total Fat: 11g, Cholesterol: 0mg, Sodium: 75mg, Total Carbohydrates: 8g, Dietary Fiber: 2.5g, Sugars: 2.5g, Protein: 4g.

40. Almond roasted veggies

Almond Roasted Veggies – A delicious roasted veggie dish made with roasted almonds to bring out the flavor.
Serving: 4
Preparation Time: 10 minutes
Ready Time: 40 minutes

Ingredients:
1 large onion, quartered
2 large carrots, peeled and chopped
2 large sweet potatoes, peeled and cubed
1 cup broccoli florets
½ cup raw almonds
4 tablespoons olive oil
Salt to taste

Instructions:
1. Preheat oven to 400°F
2. Place onion, carrots, sweet potatoes, and broccoli onto a large baking sheet.
3. Drizzle with olive oil and sprinkle with salt to taste.
4. Roast for 20 minutes, stirring once halfway through.
5. Increase oven to 415°F and add almonds to the baking sheet.
6. Roast for an additional 20 minutes until the vegetables and almonds are golden and crispy.
7. Serve and enjoy!

Nutrition Information:
Per serving: Calories 211, Carbs 22 g, Protein 5 g, Fat 13 g, Sodium 57 mg, Fiber 4 g.

41. Almond-honey-glazed carrots

Almond-honey-glazed carrots is the perfect side dish for any meal. This savory-sweet side dish features carrots glazed in a mix of honey, butter, and almond extract. Each bite is full of flavor and sure to satisfy everyone around the table!
Serving: 4
Preparation Time: 10 minutes
Ready Time: 25 minutes

Ingredients:
- 2 tablespoons butter
- 2 tablespoons honey
- 1 teaspoon almond extract
- 5 cups sliced carrots

Instructions:
1. Preheat oven to 375 degrees F (190 degrees C).
2. In a large bowl, mix together the butter, honey, and almond extract until well combined.
3. Add the carrots to the bowl and toss until evenly coated.
4. Spread the carrots on a baking sheet and bake for 25 minutes, until the carrots are tender and lightly browned.
5. Serve warm and enjoy!

Nutrition Information: 60 Calories, 5g Fat, 8g Carbohydrates, 1g Protein

42. Almond-jam thumbprint cookies

Almond-jam thumbprint cookies are a delicious and easy-to-make snack perfect for sweet tooths of all ages.

Serving: Makes 24 cookies
Preparation Time: 15 minutes
Ready Time: 1 hour

Ingredients:
- 1/2 cup butter (room temperature)
- 1/2 cup sugar
- 1/2 teaspoon almond extract
- 1 cup all-purpose flour
- 1/4 teaspoon salt
- 30-60 mL raspberry or or other type of jam
- 1/4 - 1/2 cup sliced almonds (optional)

Instructions:
- Preheat oven to 180°C (350°F).
- In a medium bowl, cream together butter and sugar until light and fluffy.
- Mix in almond extract.
- Ina separate bowl, whisk together flour and salt.
- Gradually add flour mixture to creamed mixture, mixing until just combined.
- Scoop 24 rounded teaspoonfuls of the dough onto a parchment-lined baking sheet.
- Using the back of a spoon or your thumb, create an indentation in the top of each cookie.
- Place 1/2 teaspoonful of jam into each indentation and sprinkle with almonds (optional).
- Bake for 10-12 minutes, or until golden brown.
- Let cool for 10 minutes before serving.

Nutrition Information (per cookie): 120 calories; 5g fat; 17g carbohydrates; 1.5g protein.

43. Almond-stuffed dates

Almond-Stuffed Dates
Serving: 10
Preparation Time: 5 minutes

Ready Time: 5 minutes

Ingredients:
- 10 dates
- 10 almonds
- 1 tablespoon of your desired sweetener

Instructions:
1. Cut dates open length-wise, being careful not to cut all the way through.
2. Remove the pit in the center of each date.
3. Stuff almonds into the dates.
4. Drizzle the dates with sweetener.

Nutrition Information:
Calories: 120, Total Fat: 5 g, Saturated Fat: 0.5 g, Sodium: 0 mg, Total Carbohydrates: 18 g, Dietary Fiber: 3 g, Sugars: 14 g, Protein: 3 g.

44. Almond oatmeal bowl

Almond Oatmeal Bowl
Serving: 2
Preparation time: 10 minutes
Ready time: 25 minutes

Ingredients:
-1 cup rolled oats
-2 cups almond milk
-¼ teaspoon ground cinnamon
-¼ teaspoon ground nutmeg
-½ teaspoon almond extract
-2 tablespoons honey
-⅓ cup raisons
-⅓ cup chopped slivered almonds
-2 tablespoons chia seeds

Instructions:
1. In a large pot, bring 2 cups of almond milk to a gentle boil.

2. Reduce the heat, and add in the oatmeal.

3. Stir the oatmeal constantly until it thickens and starts to bubble.

4. Add in the cinnamon, nutmeg, almond extract and honey to the pot and stir to combine.

5. Stir in the raisons, almonds and chia seeds.

6. Cook for 5-7 minutes, stirring occasionally.

7. Remove the oatmeal from the heat and let it sit for a few minutes before serving.

Nutrition Information (per serving):
-Calories: 318
-Fat: 11.8g
-Carbohydrates: 42.5g
-Protein: 8.9g

45. Almond granola

Almond granola is a simple and tasty breakfast. It's a combination of oats, nuts, honey or maple syrup, and dried fruit. It's a dish that is both lightweight and filling.
Serving: Makes 8 servings
Preparation Time: 10 minutes
Ready Time: 30 minutes

Ingredients:
- 2 cups rolled oats
- ½ cup honey or pure maple syrup
- 3 tablespoons vegetable oil
- 1 ½ teaspoon vanilla extract
- 1 cup almonds, slivered
- ½ cup dried fruit of choice

Instructions:
1. Preheat the oven to 350 degrees F.

2. In a large bowl, mix together oats, honey or maple syrup, oil and vanilla.

3. Spread the mixture on a lightly greased baking sheet.

4. Bake for 15-18 minutes, stirring once.

5. Add almonds and dried fruit. Stir.
6. Bake for another 10-12 minutes.
7. Cool the mixture before serving.

Nutrition Information:
Calories: 218, Total Fat: 9 g, Sat. Fat: 1 g, Trans Fat: 0 g, Cholesterol: 0 mg, Sodium: 0 mg, Total Carbs: 28 g, Fiber: 3 g, Sugars: 12 g, Protein: 5 g

46. Almond cherry smoothie bowl

Refreshing and creamy, this almond cherry smoothie bowl is a perfect nutritious breakfast or snack!
Serving: 2
Preparation Time: 5 minutes
Ready Time: 5 minutes

Ingredients:
• 1½ cups frozen cherries
• 1 banana, cut into chunks
• 1 teaspoon almond butter
• ½ teaspoon ground ginger
• ¼ teaspoon ground cinnamon
• 1-2 tablespoons almond milk

Instructions:
1. Place the cherries, banana, almond butter, ground ginger, ground cinnamon and 1 tablespoon of almond milk in a blender.
2. Blend the mixture until smooth, adding more almond milk if necessary.
3. Divide the smoothie between two bowls and top with desired toppings.

Nutrition Information:
Calories: 239 kcal; Fat: 5g; Carbohydrates: 50g; Protein: 3g; Sodium: 10mg; Sugar: 25g.

47. Almond-avocado toast

Almond-avocado toast is a delicious and healthy breakfast or snack option. This simple recipe combines robust crunchy almonds and smooth delicious avocados with toast for the perfect balance of flavors.
Serving: 4
Preparation time: 10 minutes
Ready time: 10 minutes

Ingredients:
- 8 slices of your favorite toast
- 2 avocados
- ¼ cup toasted almonds
- 2 tsp white wine vinegar
- Salt and pepper to taste

Instructions:
1. Preheat toaster oven or broiler.
2. Toast your toast to preferred crispness.
3. Slice avocados into thin ½ inch slices and arrange on the toast.
4. Sprinkle on almonds and season with salt and pepper.
5. Drizzle with white wine vinegar.

Nutrition Information (per serving):
Calories: 295, Fat: 16g, Protein: 6g, Carbohydrates: 33g, Sodium: 263mg.

48. Almond butter banana bread

This recipe for Almond Butter Banana Bread combines easy-to-find Ingredients to bake a delicious and unique loaf.
Serving: Makes 1 loaf, 8-10 Slices
Preparation Time: 15 minutes
Ready Time: 1 hour

Ingredients:
- 2 cups all-purpose flour
- 1 teaspoon baking soda
- 1 teaspoon baking powder

- 1/2 teaspoon kosher salt
- 1/2 cup creamy almond butter
- 2 large eggs
- 2 large bananas, mashed
- 1/2 cup packed brown sugar
- 1/2 cup almond milk
- 2 tablespoons melted coconut oil
- 2 teaspoons pure vanilla extract

Instructions:
1. Preheat oven to 350 degrees. Grease a 9"x 5" loaf pan and set aside.
2. In a large bowl, whisk together the flour, baking soda, baking powder, and salt. In a separate bowl, whisk together the almond butter, eggs, mashed bananas, brown sugar, almond milk, coconut oil, and vanilla until well combined.
3. Add the wet Ingredients to the dry Ingredients and stir until just combined.
4. Pour the batter into prepared pan and bake for 40-50 minutes until golden brown and a toothpick inserted in the center comes out clean.
5. Let bread cool for 10 minutes before transferring to a wire rack to cool completely.

Nutrition Information:
- Calories per serving: 282
- Fat: 12.8 g
- Carbohydrates: 37.0 g
- Protein: 6.8 g

49. Almond breadcrumbs

Almond Breadcrumbs is a crunchy and flavorful addition to your favorite dishes, giving them a delicious nutty flavor.
Serving: 4-6
Preparation Time: 10 mins
Ready Time: 20 mins

Ingredients:
-1 cup almonds

-1 cup plain panko breadcrumbs
-1/4 teaspoon garlic powder
-2 tablespoons olive oil
-Salt

Instructions:
1. Preheat oven to 375°F.
2. Spread the almonds out on a parchment-lined baking sheet and bake for 5 minutes until lightly toasted.
3. Let cool slightly, then place the almonds in a high-powered blender and pulse for 1-2 minutes until they're broken up into small pieces.
4. Transfer the almond pieces to a bowl and mix together with the breadcrumbs, garlic powder, oil, and salt.
5. Spread the almond-breadcrumb mixture out on the baking sheet and bake for 15 minutes, stirring half way through.
6. Let cool for 5 minutes before serving.

Nutrition Information:
Calories: 178
Fat: 15 g
Saturated Fat: 2 g
Carbohydrates: 8 g
Protein: 5 g

50. Almond pesto

Almond pesto is a delicious and nutritious sauce that is great for adding flavor to any dish. It's packed with the nutty flavor of almonds, olive oil, raw garlic, basil, and freshly grated Parmesan cheese, all combined to create a mouthwatering flavor combination.
Serving: Makes 4 servings
Preparation time: 10 minutes
Ready time: 10 minutes

Ingredients:
- 1/2 cup slivered almonds
- 1/2 cup extra-virgin olive oil
- 2 cloves of garlic, minced

- 1/2 cup packed basil leaves
- 1/2 cup freshly grated Parmesan cheese
- Salt and freshly ground black pepper to taste

Instructions:
1. Put the almonds in a food processor and process until coarsely chopped.
2. Add the remaining Ingredients and pulse until a thick paste is formed.
3. Adjust the seasoning to taste and serve.

Nutrition Information: Per Serving - 150 Calories, 13g Fat, 4g Protein, 3g Carbs, 0g Fiber

51. Almond praline ice cream

Almond praline ice cream is a delicious dessert that is perfect for warm summer days. It is creamy and sweet thanks to the almonds and the praline, which give it a unique flavor.
Serving: 4
Preparation time: 30 minutes
Ready time: 4 hours

Ingredients:
- 500ml single cream
- 4 egg yolks
- 80g sugar
- 1 teaspoon of almond extract
- 150g praline, roughly chopped

Instructions:
1. In a bowl, whisk together the cream, egg yolks, sugar, and almond extract until smooth.
2. Place the mixture in the fridge to chill for 30 minutes.
3. Put the mixture into an ice cream maker and churn according to the manufacturer's Instructions.
4. Once the ice cream is done, mix in the chopped praline.
5. Transfer the ice cream to a freezer-safe container and freeze for at least 4 hours.

Nutrition Information: Per serving - Calories: 374 kcal, Protein: 4.7 g, Carbohydrates: 19.6 g, Fat: 29.3 g

52. Almond milk and honey facial mask

Almond Milk and Honey Facial Mask
Serving: 1-2
Preparation Time: 5 minutes
Ready Time: 10-15 minutes

Ingredients:
- 2 teaspoons almond milk
- 1 teaspoon honey

Instructions:
1. In a small bowl, mix together 2 teaspoons almond milk with 1 teaspoon honey until smooth.
2. Using your fingertips, apply the mixture evenly onto your face, avoiding the eye area.
3. Leave the mask on for 10-15 minutes.
4. Rinse the mask off with warm water and pat your skin dry.

Nutrition Information:
Almond Milk: Calories per 8 ounces: 32; Protein: 1.5 to 2 g; Fat: 2.7 g; Carbohydrates: 1.7 g
Honey: Calories per 2 teaspoons: 30; Protein: 0 g; Fat: 0 g; Carbohydrates: 8.3 g

53. Almond brown sugar scrub

Almond Brown Sugar Scrub
Serving: 1 small jar
Preparation Time: 10 minutes
Ready Time: 10 minutes

Ingredients:

- 5 tablespoons of whole almonds
- 5 tablespoons of brown sugar
- 2-3 drops of almond essential oil

Instructions:
1. Preheat your oven to 375 degrees.
2. Place almonds on a baking tray and toast in the oven for 10 minutes until lightly golden.
3. Remove from the oven and allow to cool.
4. In a food processor or blender, coarsely grind the almonds.
5. Add the brown sugar and essential oil to the ground almonds and process until blended.
6. Transfer the mixture to a small jar and use as a scrub on your skin.

Nutrition Information:
Calories: 86 kcal, Fat: 4g, Carbohydrates: 10g, Protein: 2g, Sodium: 2mg

54. Almond vanilla sugar scrub

Almond vanilla sugar scrub is a beautifully scented and moisturizing exfoliator that will help keep your skin feeling soft and smooth.
Serving: Makes 4-6 portions
Preparation Time: 10 mins
Ready Time: 10 mins

Ingredients:
- 1 cup fine granulated sugar
- 2 tablespoons almond oil
- 1 teaspoon vanilla extract

Instructions:
1. Put 1 cup of fine granulated sugar in a medium bowl.
2. Add 2 tablespoons of almond oil and 1 teaspoon of vanilla extract to the bowl.
3. Use a rubber spatula and mix the Ingredients together until fully combined.
4. Transfer the scrub to an air-tight container.

Nutrition Information:
Calories per serving: 175
Carbohydrates: 36 g
Protein: 0 g
Fat: 6 g
Saturated fat: 0.5 g
Sugars: 33 g
Sodium: 1 mg
Cholesterol: 0 mg

55. Almond coconut body butter

Indulge your skin with this homemade almond coconut body butter recipe! It's naturally moisturizing, luxurious and will leave your skin feeling silky smooth.
Serving: Approximately 10 oz of body butter
Preparation Time: 10 minutes
Ready Time: 4 hours

Ingredients:
- 1 cup unrefined coconut oil
- ½ cup almond oil
- ½ cup cocoa butter
- 30 drops sweet orange essential oil
- 15 drops vanilla essential oil

Instructions:
1. Using a double boiler, over low heat, melt the coconut oil, almond oil, and cocoa butter. Stir occasionally until completely melted and combined.
2. Remove from heat and let cool until the mixture is still liquid but no longer hot.
3. Add the essential oils and mix well.
4. Transfer the mixture to a shallow pie tin or tupperware container and place in the refrigerator for 4 hours or until solid.
5. Remove from refrigerator and with an electric hand mixer, whip the body butter until light and fluffy.
6. Transfer into glass jars with airtight lid and store in a cool, dry place.

Nutrition Information:
Calories: 106 Calories,
Carbohydrates: 2.4 g
Fat: 11.5 g
Protein: 0.3 g

56. Almond milk soap

Almond Milk Soap - a luxurious and nourishing homemade soap that is perfect for those with sensitive skin. This soap is made with 100% natural and organic Ingredients, is vegan and cruelty-free. It is light and fragrant, and leaves the skin feeling soft and smooth.
Serving: 10 bars of soap
Preparation Time: 30 minutes
Ready Time: 6 to 8 hours

Ingredients:
• 1/2 cup almond oil
• 1/2 cup coconut oil
• 1/4 cup castor oil
• 2 tablespoons shea butter
• 2 tablespoons beeswax
• 2 tablespoons almond milk
• 2-3 tablespoons lye
• Essential oils of choice

Instructions:
1. Measure all oils and butter into a glass bowl and melt in microwave for about 1 minute.
2. Measure and mix together the lye and almond milk in a shallow bowl.
3. Slowly add the lye and almond milk mixture to the melted oils and mix until it begins to thicken.
4. Add essential oils and mix thoroughly.
5. Pour the soap mixture into a silicone mold and let it set for 6-8 hours.
6. Gently remove the soap from the mold and allow to harden for another few days before using.

Nutrition Information:
Almond Milk Soap is naturally high in vitamins and minerals that help nourish and protect the skin. It contains healthy fats and antioxidants from the almond oil, coconut oil, shea butter, and beeswax, as well as nutrients from the almond milk.

57. Almond milk bath salts

Relaxing and indulgent, this almond-scented almond milk bath salts recipe is perfect for a calming soak.
Serving: 3-4
Preparation Time: 10 minutes
Ready Time: 10 minutes

Ingredients:
- 2 cups Epsom salt
- 2 tablespoons baking soda
- 10 drops almond essential oil
- 1 tablespoon almond extract
- 2 teaspoons arrowroot powder
- 1/4 cup light almond milk

Instructions:
1. In a large bowl, combine Epsom salt and baking soda.
2. Whisk in almond oil, almond extract, arrowroot powder and almond milk until well combined.
3. Divide the mixture among 3-4 small mason jars and screw lids on loosely.
4. Store in a cool, dry place away from light and heat.

Nutrition Information: Per serving, almond milk bath salts contains 0 calories, 0 g fat, 0 g of sodium, and 0 g of sugar.

58. Almond nail oil

Almond Nail Oil is the perfect solution for softer, more beautiful cuticles. With a blend of natural Ingredients like almond oil, jojoba oil,

and tea tree oil, this nourishing oil helps maintain the health of nails and cuticles.
Serving: 1-2 Drops of Oil Per Nail
Preparation Time: 1 Minute
Ready Time: Instant

Ingredients:
- 1 tablespoon almond oil
- 2 tablespoons jojoba oil
- 5 drops tea tree oil

Instructions:
1. Combine almond oil, jojoba oil, and tea tree oil in a small bowl.
2. Stir until all Ingredients are evenly combined.
3. Dip a Q-tip in the mixture and apply 1-2 drops of oil to each nail.
4. Massage the oil into the nail and cuticle area.

Nutrition Information:
Calories: 148 kcal, Carbohydrates: 0 g, Protein: 0 g, Fat: 17 g, Cholesterol: 0 mg, Sodium: 0 mg, Potassium: 0 mg, Vitamin A: 0 IU, Vitamin C: 0 mg, Calcium: 0 mg, Iron: 0 mg.

59. Almond facial serum

Almond Facial Serum
This almond facial serum is naturally infused with the nourishing, powerful properties of almond extract. It locks in moisture to keep skin soft and smooth while balancing your complexion. The nourishing natural extracts provide a gentle boost of antioxidant protection, leaving skin looking fresh, vibrant, and healthy.
Serving: 1
Preparation Time: 10 minutes
Ready Time: 10 minutes

Ingredients:
- 1 tablespoon almond extract
- 2 drops of lavender essential oil
- 2 drops of sweet orange essential oil

- 1 teaspoon jojoba oil
- 1 teaspoon Argan oil

Instructions:
1. In a small bowl, stir together the almond extract, lavender essential oil, sweet orange essential oil, jojoba oil, and Argan oil.
2. Mix the oils until all Ingredients are evenly incorporated.
3. Apply a small amount of the serum onto the skin.
4. Massage the serum into the skin in a circular motion.
5. Allow the serum to absorb into the skin, usually 15-20 minutes.

Nutrition Information (per serving):
Calories: 27 kcal
Fat: 2.4 g
Carbohydrates: 0.1 g
Protein: 0.2 g

60. Almond shampoo

Almond shampoo is a natural, nourishing way to care for your hair without using sulfates or other harsh Ingredients. This blend of Ingredients helps to deeply nourish your scalp and hair, leaving them feeling soft and healthy.
Serving: 6 – 8
Preparation Time: 10 minutes
Ready Time: 10 minutes

Ingredients:
- 2 tablespoons almond oil
- 2 tablespoons aloe vera
- 1 teaspoon vitamin E oil
- 1/4 cup liquid castile soap

Instructions:
1. In a bowl, add almond oil, aloe vera, and vitamin E oil. Mix well.
2. Add liquid castile soap and mix until a creamy shampoo is formed.
3. Transfer the mixture to a bottle and store it in a cool, dry place.

Nutrition Information:
Almond shampoo is a nutrient-rich shampoo that provides many benefits for hair health, including: essential fatty acids, vitamin E, protein, minerals, and micronutrients. Additionally, almond oil can help strengthen the hair and scalp, while aloe vera helps to soothe irritation.

61. Almond conditioner

Almond conditioner is a nourishing, all natural DIY conditioner made from almond oil that helps to lock in moisture and repair damaged hair strands.
Servings: Around 4-6
Preparation Time: 15 mins
Ready Time: 45 mins

Ingredients:
- ¼ cup almond oil
- ½ cup water
- ¼ cup honey
- 1 tablespoon lemon juice

Instructions:
1. In a bowl, mix together the almond oil, water, honey and lemon juice.
2. Stir everything together until combined.
3. Apply the mixture to your damp hair, from the roots to the tips.
4. Put on a shower cap and leave the almond conditioner in for about 45 minutes.
5. Wash your hair with shampoo and water as usual.

Nutrition Information:
Calories: 102, Protein: 0g, Carbohydrates: 12.1g, Fat: 6.8g, Cholesterol: 0mg, Sodium: 8mg, Fiber: 0.2g.

62. Almond hair oil

Almond Hair Oil is an easy recipe that promotes hair growth and maintains scalp health. It's a great natural conditioner that is great for all hair types.
Serving:
Makes enough for one use.
Preparation Time:
5 minutes
Ready Time:
5 minutes

Ingredients:
- 2 tablespoons of almond oil
- 1 tablespoon of jojoba oil

Instructions:
1. In a small bowl, mix together the almond oil and jojoba oil.
2. Apply the oil blend to the scalp, gently massaging it in.
3. Leave the oil on the scalp for an hour or overnight.
4. Wash your hair with shampoo as usual.

Nutrition Information:
Serving Size: 1
Calories: 126 cal
Total Fat: 14 g
Sodium: 0 mg
Carbohydrates: 0 g
Protein: 0 g

63. Almond bread pudding

Almond Bread Pudding
Serving: 8
Preparation Time: 15 minutes
Ready Time: 45 minutes

Ingredients:
- 6 cups of cubed French bread
- 2 cups of whole milk

- 4 eggs
- 2 tsp almond extract
- 1/4 cup white sugar
- 2 tsp ground cinnamon
- 2 tbsp butter
- 1/2 cup toasted almond flakes

Instructions:
1. Preheat oven to 350 degrees F (175 degrees C). Grease a 9x13 inch baking dish.
2. Place cubed French bread in the dish.
3. In a large bowl, beat together milk, eggs, almond extract, sugar, and cinnamon. Pour mixture over bread cubes. Dot top with butter. Sprinkle almond flakes over top.
4. Bake in preheated oven for 45 minutes, or until a knife inserted in the center comes out clean.

Nutrition Information:
Per Serving: 8 servings
Calories: 220 kcal
Carbohydrates: 27 g
Protein: 8 g
Fat: 7 g
Saturated fat: 3 g
Cholesterol: 76 mg
Sodium: 349 mg
Potassium: 149 mg
Fiber: 1.5 g
Sugar: 9.5 g

64. Almond quinoa salad

This Almond Quinoa Salad is a light and nutritious meal for lunch or dinner. It's full of protein, fiber, and healthy fats and can be eaten as a main dish or a side.
Serving: 6
Preparation time: 5 minutes
Ready time: 15 minutes

Ingredients:

 1 cup quinoa, rinsed
4 cups water
1/4 cup almonds, sliced
1/4 cup olive oil
2 tablespoons lemon juice
1 red bell pepper, finely chopped
1 red onion, finely chopped
1 teaspoon garlic, minced
1 teaspoon oregano
Salt to taste

Instructions:

1. In a medium saucepan, bring quinoa and water to a boil. Reduce heat to low and simmer for 15 minutes.
2. In a medium bowl, combine almonds, olive oil, lemon juice, red bell pepper, red onion, garlic, oregano, and salt.
3. When the quinoa is done, add it to the bowl with almonds and other Ingredients and mix everything together.
4. Serve as is or chilled.

Nutrition Information:

Calories: 250, Fat: 13g, Protein: 13g, Fiber: 5g, Carbs: 24g

65. Almond chicken salad

Almond Chicken Salad is an easy, healthy meal that is perfect for a summer lunch or light dinner. It's packed with flavor and nutrition, thanks to the combination of crunchy almonds, sweet cranberries, tender chicken, and a tangy lemon-poppy seed dressing.
Serving: 4
Preparation Time: 15 minutes
Ready Time: 15 minutes

Ingredients:

- 3 cups cooked and shredded chicken
- ½ cup diced celery

- ½ cup sliced almonds
- ½ cup dried cranberries
- 2 tablespoons minced green onion
- ⅓ cup plain Greek yogurt
- 2 tablespoons mayonnaise
- 2 teaspoons fresh lemon juice
- 1 teaspoon sugar
- Pinch of salt
- 1 teaspoon poppy seed

Instructions:
1. In a medium bowl, combine shredded chicken, celery, almonds, cranberries, and green onion.
2. In a separate bowl, whisk together yogurt, mayonnaise, lemon juice, sugar, salt, and poppy seeds.
3. Pour dressing over chicken mixture and toss until everything is thoroughly coated.
4. Divide salad among 4 plates and serve.

Nutrition Information:(per serving)
Calories: 295
Total Fat: 10g
Cholesterol: 62mg
Sodium: 385mg
Carbohydrates: 21g
Sugar: 9g
Protein: 29g

66. Almond berry salad

Almond Berry Salad
Serving: 4
Preparation Time: 15 minutes
Ready Time: 15 minutes

Ingredients:
2 cups baby spinach
2 cups fresh raspberries

2 cups fresh blueberries
1/3 cup slivered almonds
1/4 cup feta cheese
1/4 cup olive oil
1/4 cup balsamic vinaigrette

Instructions:
1. In a large bowl, combine the baby spinach, fresh raspberries, fresh blueberries, slivered almonds, and feta cheese.
2. Drizzle the olive oil and balsamic vinaigrette over the salad and toss to combine.
3. Serve and enjoy.

Nutrition Information (per serving):
Calories: 218
Fat: 16 g
Carbohydrates: 18 g
Protein: 5 g

67. Almond stuffed zucchini

Almond stuffed zucchini is a simple vegetarian dish that will please everyone at the dinner table. Combining the freshness of zucchini, the nuttiness of almonds, and the piquancy of spices makes for a flavorful and nutritious meal.
Serving: 4
Preparation time: 10 minutes
Ready time: 30 minutes

Ingredients:
• 4 large zucchini
• 2 cups almond flour
• ½ cup roasted ground sunflower seeds
• 2 tablespoons olive oil
• 2 tablespoons chopped coriander
• ½ teaspoon cumin powder
• ½ teaspoon red chili flakes
• Salt and pepper to taste

Instructions:

1. Preheat the oven to 350°F and lightly grease a baking sheet.
2. Slice the zucchini into thick rounds and place them on the baking sheet.
3. Mix the almond flour, sunflower seeds, olive oil, coriander, cumin, chili flakes, salt, and pepper in a large bowl.
4. Fill the zucchini rounds with the almond mixture.
5. Bake for 25 to 30 minutes, or until the tops are golden-brown.

Nutrition Information (per serving):
- Calories: 224
- Fat: 17 g
- Carbs: 10 g
- Protein: 7 g

68. Almond stuffed mushrooms

Almond Stuffed Mushrooms - a delectable combination of aromatic mushrooms and creamy almond filling, these mushrooms are sure to be a hit!
Serving: 4
Preparation Time: 10 minutes
Ready Time: 45 minutes

Ingredients:
- 12 Whole Mushrooms
- ¼ Cup of Almonds
- 1 Tablespoon of Olive Oil
- 2 Tablespoons of Chopped Parsley
- 2 Tablespoons of Chopped Green Onion
- ½ Teaspoon of Salt
- ¼ Teaspoon of Ground Black Pepper

Instructions:

1. Preheat the oven to 400°F.
2. Remove the stems from the mushrooms, and place the caps on a large baking sheet.

3. Finely process the almonds in a food processor until a crumbly texture forms.

4. Heat the olive oil in a skillet over medium heat. Add the parsley, green onion, salt, and pepper. Stir until combined.

5. Pour the almond mixture into the skillet and stir until it is heated through and combined with the other Ingredients.

6. Stuff each mushroom cap with the almond mixture.

7. Bake the mushrooms in the preheated oven for 30 minutes.

Nutrition Information:
•Calories: 127 kcal
•Protein: 3.3g
•Carbohydrates: 6.4g
•Fat: 10.4g
•Sugar:0.9g
•Sodium: 389mg

69. Almond stuffed chicken

Almond Stuffed Chicken
Serving: 4-6
Preparation Time: 10 minutes
Ready Time: 60 minutes

Ingredients:
- 6 boneless, skinless chicken breasts
- 4 tablespoons butter
- 2 cloves garlic, minced
- 1 cup almond slivers
- Salt, to taste
- Pepper, to taste
- 1/4 cup white wine

Instructions:
1. Preheat oven to 375F.

2. In a large skillet, melt butter over medium heat. Add garlic and almond slivers and cook until toasted, about 2 minutes.

3. Season chicken breasts with salt and pepper. Place into a baking dish.

4. Top each chicken breast with almond slivers and spread evenly over the surface.
5. Pour white wine over chicken breasts.
6. Bake for 45 minutes or until chicken is cooked through.

Nutrition Information:
Calories: 348, Fat: 17g, Carbs: 7g, Protein: 33g

70. Almond-stuffed pork chops

Almond-Stuffed Pork Chops is a savory main dish that packs a flavorful punch. Tender pork chops are brushed with a combination of spices and filled with a creamy almond paste before being cooked to perfection. This delicious dish is sure to satisfy everyone at the table!
Serving: 4
Preparation Time: 10 mins
Ready Time: 40 mins

Ingredients:
• 4 pork chops, 1/2-inch thick and bone-in
• 1 tsp olive oil
• 1 garlic clove, minced
• 1 tsp fresh parsley, chopped
• 1/4 cup almonds, chopped
• 2 tbsp cream cheese
• 2 tsp Dijon mustard
• 2 tsp Worcestershire sauce
• Salt and pepper, to taste

Instructions:
1. Preheat oven to 350°F.
2. Heat olive oil in a small skillet over medium heat. Add garlic and parsley, and sauté for 1 to 2 minutes or until fragrant.
3. In a medium bowl, combine almonds, cream cheese, Dijon mustard, and Worcestershire sauce.
4. Cut a pocket in each pork chop and fill with almond mixture. Secure with toothpicks.

5. Place pork chops onto a baking sheet and season with salt and pepper, as desired.
6. Bake for 30 to 40 minutes, or until pork is cooked through and internal temperature has reached 160°F.

Nutrition Information:
Serving size: 1 stuffed pork chop
Calories: 259
Fat: 17.3 g
Carbohydrate: 1.7 g
Protein: 23 g
Sodium: 157 mg

71. Almond-herb crusted lamb

Try this delicious, fragrant and flavorful recipe for almond-herbs crusted lamb, featuring an herb rub and rolled in almond slivers. Servings: 4 Preparation time: 20 minutes Ready time: 1 hour 20 minutes

Ingredients:
- 1 ½ lbs Lamb loin
- 2 cloves minced garlic
- 2 Tbsp olive oil
- 2 Tbsp chopped fresh thyme
- 2 Tbsp chopped fresh rosemary
- 2 Tbsp chopped fresh oregano
- 2 Tbsp grated Parmesan
- 2 Tbsp almond slivers

Instructions:
1. Preheat oven to 375°F. Line a baking sheet with parchment paper.
2. Rub garlic, olive oil and herbs over the lamb loin.
3. Roll the lamb loin in the almond slivers and Parmesan, pressing them in to adhere.
4. Place the coated lamb loin on the parchment-lined baking sheet.
5. Bake in preheated oven for 55-60 minutes or until desired doneness is reached.
6. Let the cooked lamb rest for 10 minutes before slicing and serving.

Nutrition Information: Per serving: (Based on 4 servings): 304cal, 15g fat, 7g protein, 6g carbohydrates, 2g fiber.

72. Almond-crusted beef tenderloin

Almond-crusted Beef Tenderloin
A succulent and sophisticated dish, the almond-crusted beef tenderloin is perfect for special occasions. It has a crunchy texture and is packed with flavour.
Serving: 8
Preparation Time: 30 minutes
Ready Time: 1 1/2 hours

Ingredients:
- 2-3lbs of beef tenderloin
- 2 Tablespoons of yellow mustard
- 1 cup of finely ground almonds
- 2 large eggs
- 1 teaspoon of paprika
- 1 teaspoon of garlic powder
- 2 teaspoon of onion powder
- Freshly ground black pepper
- Sea salt

Instructions:
1. Preheat oven to 300F.
2. Rub beef tenderloin with the mustard.
3. Mix together the almond powder, paprika, garlic powder, onion powder, freshly ground black pepper, and salt in a shallow bowl until combined.
4. Beat the eggs in a separate shallow bowl.
5. Dip the beef tenderloin in the egg mixture, and then roll it in the almond mixture until completely covered.
6. Place the beef on a roasting tin and cook in the pre-heated oven for 1 1/4 hours.
7. When cooked, remove from the oven and rest for 5 minutes before serving.

Nutrition Information:
Calories: 432 kcal
Carbohydrates: 6g
Protein: 28g
Fat: 30g
Saturated Fat: 7g
Sodium: 144mg

73. Almond-crusted tofu

Almond-crusted tofu is a tasty and nutritious vegan-friendly meal that can be served in just about any setting. With cruncy almonds and pan-seared tofu, this dish will be sure to please the palate.
Serving: 4
Preparation time: 10 minutes
Ready time: 30 minutes

Ingredients:
- 14 ounces extra-firm tofu, pressed for at least 15 minutes
- 1/4 teaspoon garlic powder
- 1/4 teaspoon onion powder
- 1/4 teaspoon salt
- 1/2 teaspoon smoked paprika
- 1/4 teaspoon freshly ground black pepper
- 2 cups slivered almonds
- 1/2 cup all-purpose flour
- 2 tablespoons nutritional yeast
- 2 tablespoons olive oil

Instructions:
1. Preheat oven to 375°F (190°C). Line a large baking sheet with parchment paper.
2. Cut pressed tofu into quarters. Place in a shallow bowl and sprinkle with garlic powder, onion powder, salt, smoked paprika, and black pepper. Gently stir to coat.
3. In a separate bowl, combine almonds, flour, and nutritional yeast.
4. Heat the olive oil in a large skillet over medium-high heat.

5. Dip each tofu quarter into the almond mixture, making sure it is evenly coated.
6. Place the coated tofu quarters onto the prepared baking sheet and bake for 15 minutes.
7. After baking, place the tofu pieces in the hot oil and cook for an additional 3-4 minutes, flipping once, until golden brown.

Nutrition Information: Per serving (1/4 of the recipe): Calories: 433, Fat: 21.7g, Carbohydrates: 24.4g, Protein: 31.2g, Sodium: 227mg.

74. Almond-crusted tempeh

Almond-crusted tempeh is a delicious and nutritious vegan option as a main dish. This simple and versatile recipe is flavourful and easy to prepare.
Serving: 4
Preparation Time: 15 mins
Ready Time: 40 mins

Ingredients:
• 8 ounces of tempeh (two 4-ounce pieces), cut into ½-inch thick slices
• ½ cup almond meal
• 2 tablespoons white sesame seeds
• 1 teaspoon smoked paprika
• ½ teaspoon garlic powder
• ¼ teaspoon cayenne pepper
• 1 teaspoon sea salt
• 4 tablespoons of melted coconut oil

Instructions:
1. Preheat oven to 400°F (204°C)
2. Line a baking sheet with parchment paper
3. In a bowl, mix almond meal, sesame seeds, paprika, garlic powder, cayenne pepper, and sea salt
4. Dip each slice of tempeh into the almond meal mixture, making sure to coat both sides.

5. Arrange tempeh slices on the baking sheet, and brush each slice with coconut oil
6. Bake in the oven for 25 minutes, flipping once after 15 minutes
7. Enjoy!

Nutrition Information (per serving):
• 320 calories
• 20g fat
• 8g carbohydrates
• 24g protein

75. Almond milk tea

Almond Milk Tea: This classic Chinese tea, made with milk and sweet almonds, is sure to please any tea lover.
Serving: 1
Preparation Time: 10 minutes
Ready Time: 10 minutes

Ingredients:
- 1 cup of almond milk
- 2 tsp of honey
- 2 tsp of loose-leaf black tea
- 2 tbsp of blanched almonds

Instructions:
1. Boil 1 cup of almond milk over medium-low heat in a small saucepan.
2. Add the honey and stir until it has dissolved.
3. Add the loose-leaf black tea and blanched almonds and allow the mixture to boil for 1 minute.
4. Remove from heat and strain the mixture into a mug.

Nutrition Information (per serving):
Calories – 300 kcal
Fat – 13 g
Carbohydrates – 34 g
Fiber – 3 g
Protein – 8 g

76. Almond fudge

Almond Fudge is an old-fashioned favorite that is easy to make and always delicious. It's a classic no-bake treat that's creamy, chocolaty, and crunchy from the nuts.
Serving: Makes 16 pieces
Preparation Time: 15 minutes
Ready Time: 1 hour (plus 2 hours chill time)

Ingredients:
- 1/4 cup butter
- 2 1/2 cups powdered sugar
- 2/3 cup cocoa powder
- 2 tablespoons half-and-half
- 1 teaspoon vanilla extract
- 1/4 teaspoon salt
- 1 cup toasted sliced almonds

Instructions:
1. Grease an 8-inch square baking pan and set aside.
2. In a large saucepan, melt the butter over medium-low heat.
3. Add in the powdered sugar, cocoa powder, half-and-half, vanilla extract, and salt. Stir until everything is combined.
4. Remove the pan from the heat and fold in the toasted almonds, stirring until everything is mixed together.
5. Pour the fudge into the prepared pan and spread it evenly.
6. Refrigerate for at least two hours before cutting.

Nutrition Information: Per 3-inch piece (55g): 154 calories, 7.7g fat, 19.4g carbohydrates, 1g fiber, 2.5g protein

77. Almond toffee

Almond Toffee is a classic, crunchy candy that's simply irresistible. It's made with almonds, butter, sugar, and water and is quite easy to make.
Serving: 8

Preparation Time: 25 minutes
Ready Time: 45 minutes

Ingredients:
- 2 cups chopped, blanched almonds
- 1 cup butter
- 1/2 cup granulated white sugar
- 1/4 cup water

Instructions:
1. Preheat oven to 300 degrees F and line a baking sheet with parchment paper.
2. In a medium saucepan, melt butter over low heat.
3. Add the chopped almonds, sugar, and water and stir to combine.
4. Increase the heat to medium-high and stir constantly for about 12 minutes, until the mixture is thick and golden-brown.
5. Pour the toffee mixture onto the parchment-lined baking pan and spread evenly with a wooden spoon.
6. Bake for 20 minutes in preheated oven, until golden brown.
7. Remove the toffee from the oven and allow it to cool before breaking into pieces.

Nutrition Information: Per serving (1 slice), Almond Toffee contains 330 calories, 9 grams of fat, 5 grams of protein and 58 grams of carbohydrates.

78. Almond brittle popcorn

Almond Brittle Popcorn
Serving: 6
Preparation Time: 10 minutes
Ready Time: 25 minutes

Ingredients:
- 1/2 cup corn syrup
- 1/2 cup packed light-brown sugar
- 1/4 teaspoon baking soda
- 1/4 teaspoon almond extract

- 2 tablespoons butter, melted
- 6 cups popped popcorn
- 1/2 cup sliced almonds
- Pinch of salt

Instructions:
1. Preheat oven to 275°F. Line a rimmed baking sheet with parchment.
2. In a medium saucepan, bring corn syrup, sugar, and salt to a boil over medium heat, stirring with a wooden spoon to dissolve sugar. Boil until a candy thermometer registers 285°F, about 12 minutes.
3. Remove from heat; stir in baking soda, almond extract, and melted butter. Add popped popcorn and almonds, stirring to coat.
4. Transfer popcorn mixture to the baking sheet. Bake, stirring a couple of times, until brittle is golden and almonds are lightly toasted, about 15 minutes.
5. Let cool completely, then break into pieces.

Nutrition Information: Per serving (1/6 of recipe): 250 calories; 15.0 g fat; 28.6 g carbohydrates; 3.4 g protein; 0.6 mg sodium; 11.2 g sugars.

79. Almond granulated sugar

This deliciously sweet almond-granulated sugar is the perfect addition to any sweet dish. It adds a unique flavor to desserts and baked goods, while adding a crunchy texture.
Serving: Makes about 2 cups of Almond-Granulated Sugar
Preparation Time: 10 minutes
Ready Time: 10 minutes

Ingredients:
- 3 cups almond meal/flour
- 1/4 cup granulated sugar

Instructions:
1. Preheat oven to 350°F.
2. Place almond meal and sugar in a large bowl. Using a whisk or spoon, combine the Ingredients until they are completely combined.

3. Line a baking sheet with parchment paper and spread the mixture evenly on the parchment.

4. Place the baking sheet into the oven and bake for 10 minutes or till golden in color.

5. Take out of the oven and let it cool.

6. Once cool, place the mixture into a food processor or blender and blend for 15 to 30 seconds.

7. Store in an airtight container until ready to use.

Nutrition Information (per serving):
Calories: 137
Fat: 8.7g
Carbohdyrates: 12.2g
Protein: 4.1g

80. Almond paste

Almond paste is a delicious, sweet paste made from ground almonds, sugar, and egg whites. It has a silky texture and nutty flavor that makes it perfect to use as a glaze, filling, or topping for desserts and pastries.
Serving: Approximately 10
Preparation time: 20 minutes
Ready time: 45 minutes

Ingredients:
- 2 cups almond meal
- ¾ cup sugar
- 2 egg whites
- 2 teaspoons almond extract

Instructions:
1. Preheat oven to 350 degrees F.

2. In a medium bowl, mix together the almond meal, sugar, egg whites, and almond extract.

3. Grease a baking dish with butter or non-stick spray.

4. Pour the almond paste mixture into the baking dish and spread it out evenly.

5. Bake in preheated oven for 45 minutes, or until the top of the almond paste is golden brown.
6. Allow almond paste to cool completely before serving.

Nutrition Information: 1 serving (approx. 28g) contains 70 calories, 4.5g fat, 4.5g carbohydrates, 1g protein, and 55mg sodium.

81. Almond hummus

Almond Hummus: This unique and flavorful dip combines roasted almonds and traditional hummus Ingredients. Rich and creamy, it is perfect for entertaining or as a flavorful snack.
Serving: 4
Preparation Time: 15 minutes
Ready Time: 15 minutes

Ingredients:
• 2 cloves garlic
• 2 cups cooked chickpeas
• ¼ cup tahini
• ¼ cup fresh squeezed lemon juice
• ⅓ cup roasted almonds
• 2 tablespoons olive oil
• Salt and pepper, to taste
• Fresh herbs, such as parsley or dill

Instructions:
1. Combine two cloves of garlic with the two cups of cooked chickpeas in the bowl of a food processor.
2. Add tahini, lemon juice, and roasted almonds to the mixture.
3. Pulse the Ingredients together until the hummus is creamy.
4. Add olive oil and salt and pepper to taste.
5. Blend until desired consistency is achieved.
6. Transfer the almond hummus to a bowl and garnish with fresh herbs.

Nutrition Information:
Each serving of almond hummus contains approximately 170 calories, 4.5 grams of fat, 28 grams of carbohydrates, and 8 grams of protein.

82. Almond stuffed peppers

Almond Stuffed Peppers
Serving: 4-5
Preparation Time: 15 minutes
Ready Time: 40 minutes

Ingredients:
- 8 red bell peppers
- 2 tablespoons olive oil
- 2 teaspoons ground coriander
- 1 teaspoon ground cumin
- 2 cloves garlic, minced
- 1 large onion, diced
- 1 pound ground beef
- 1 and ½ cups cooked white rice
- 1 cup slivered almonds or sliced almonds
- Salt and pepper, to taste

Instructions:
1. Preheat the oven to 350°F.
2. Use a knife to remove the tops, cores, and seeds of the bell peppers. Set aside.
3. Heat a large skillet over medium-high heat.
4. Add in the olive oil.
5. Add in the coriander, cumin, garlic, and onion.
6. Cook for 6 minutes, or until softened.
7. Add in the ground beef, and cook until crumbled and browned.
8. Add in the cooked rice.
9. Remove skillet from heat and mix in the slivered almonds.
10. Place the peppers in a baking dish.
11. Stuff each pepper with the filling.
12. Bake uncovered for 35-45 minutes.

Nutrition Information:
Calories: 541
Fat: 33.2g

Protein: 23.2g
Carbs: 41.3g
Fiber: 5.2g
Sugar: 8.5g

83. Almond gravy

Almond Gravy
Serving: 10 servings
Preparation Time: 10 minutes
Ready Time: 25 minutes

Ingredients:
• 2 tablespoons cornstarch
• 2 teaspoon vegetable oil
• 2 tablespoons butter
• 2 cups vegetable broth
• 1 tablespoon parsley
• 1 tablespoon soy sauce
• 2 tablespoons almond butter
• Salt and pepper, to taste

Instructions:
1. In a small bowl, mix the cornstarch and vegetable oil together until combined.
2. In a medium saucepan, heat the butter until melted.
3. Add the cornstarch mixture to the pan and whisk together.
4. Gradually add the vegetable broth and stir until smooth.
5. Bring to a low boil and then reduce the heat to low.
6. Add the parsley, soy sauce, almond butter, salt, and pepper. Simmer for 15 minutes or until thickened.
7. Serve warm.

Nutrition Information:
• Calories: 90
• Total Fat: 7g
• Saturated Fat: 2g
• Trans Fat: 0g

- Cholesterol: 5mg
- Sodium: 220mg
- Carbohydrates: 8g
- Fiber: 1g
- Sugar: 2g
- Protein: 2g

84. Almond rice pudding

Almond Rice Pudding
Serving: 4
Preparation Time: 15 minutes
Ready Time: 2 hours

Ingredients:
- 1 cup uncooked long-grain white rice
- 2 1/2 cups milk
- 1/4 cup ground almonds
- 2 tablespoons sugar
- 1 teaspoon almond extract
- 1/4 teaspoon salt
- 1/2 teaspoon vanilla extract

Instructions:
1. In a medium saucepan, combine the rice, milk, ground almonds, sugar, almond extract, salt and vanilla extract.
2. Bring the mixture to a boil over medium-high heat.
3. Reduce the heat and simmer, stirring occasionally, for about 18 minutes, or until the rice is tender.
4. Remove the pan from the heat and let cool for about 10 minutes.
5. Divide the pudding among 4 serving dishes and let cool to room temperature.

Nutrition Information:
Calories: 236
 fat: 5 g
 protein: 6 g
 carbohydrates: 40 g

sodium: 191 mg

85. Almond quiche

Almond Quiche
Serving: 6-8
Preparation Time: 20 minutes
Ready Time: 45 minutes

Ingredients:
-1 unbaked 9-inch frozen deep-dish pie shell
-2 tablespoons butter
-3/4 cup sliced almonds
-3 eggs, slightly beaten
-1/2 cup half-and-half
-2 tablespoons honey
-1/4 teaspoon ground cinnamon
-1/4 teaspoon ground nutmeg
-Dash of salt

Instructions:
1. Preheat oven to 375°F (190°C).
2. Place pie shell on a baking sheet.
3. In a medium saucepan over medium heat, melt butter. Add almonds and stir until lightly toasted. Remove from heat and set aside.
4. In a medium bowl combine eggs, half-and-half, honey, cinnamon, nutmeg and salt. Stir until blended.
5. Sprinkle toasted almonds in bottom of pie shell.
6. Pour egg mixture over almonds.
7. Bake in preheated oven for 30-45 minutes, or until a knife inserted in the center comes out clean.

Nutrition Information:
Serving Size 1 slice
Calories 229.9 Calories from Fat 151
Total Fat 16.8g Saturated Fat 5.7g
Cholesterol 70.7mg Sodium 365.4mg
Total Carbohydrates 12.3g Dietary Fiber 0.7g

Sugars 6.4g Protein 7.6g

86. Almond-stuffed crepes

Almond-stuffed crepes are a classic French treat. They are light and airy crepes filled with a sweet almond paste and topped with a creamy glaze. They are perfect for breakfast, brunch, dessert, or as a snack.
Serving: Makes 10 crepes
Preparation Time: 15 minutes
Ready Time: 25 minutes

Ingredients:
- 2 eggs
- ½ cup all-purpose flour
- 2 tablespoons butter, melted
- ½ cup milk
- 2 tablespoons sugar
- ¼ teaspoon salt
- 2 tablespoons brandy
- 2 tablespoons almond butter
- ¼ cup confectioner's sugar
- ¼ teaspoon almond extract

Instructions:
1. In a large bowl, whisk together the eggs, flour, butter, milk, sugar, and salt until smooth.
2. Heat a crepe pan or nonstick skillet over medium heat. Brush the pan lightly with butter.
3. Ladle two tablespoons of batter into the center of the pan and then swirl around to evenly coat the bottom of the pan.
4. Cook for 2 minutes or until golden brown, flip with a spatula and cook for 1 additional minute. Assure that the center of the crepe is cooked through.
5. Place the crepe on a cutting board and spread the almond butter over the entire surface.
6. Roll the crepe up, forming a cylinder and transfer to a parchment lined baking sheet.

7. In a small bowl, whisk together the confectioner's sugar, almond extract, and 1 tablespoon of water until smooth.
8. Drizzle the glaze over each crepe. For best results, brush the glaze evenly over each roll.
9. Serve warm.

Nutrition Information: per serving (1 crepe): 108 calories, 5 g fat, 12 g carbohydrates, 2 g protein, 1 g fiber.

87. Almond-stuffed French toast

Sweet and crunchy Almond-stuffed French toast topped with powdered sugar and a drizzle of honey is a decadent breakfast treat for the whole family.
Serving: 6
Preparation Time: 10 minutes
Ready Time: 25 minutes

Ingredients:
- 12 pieces of bread
- 2 eggs
- 1/2 teaspoon vanilla extract
- 1/4 cup of honey
- 2 cups of chopped almonds
- Powdered sugar
- 1 teaspoon of ground cinnamon
- 1/2 teaspoon of ground nutmeg
- 2 tablespoons of butter

Instructions:
1. Preheat oven to 350 degrees F (175 degrees C).
2. Cut a slit in each piece of bread.
3. In a large bowl, beat together the eggs, 1/4 cup honey, vanilla extract, ground nutmeg, and ground cinnamon.
4. Spread chopped almonds inside each slice of bread.
5. Melt butter in a large skillet over medium – low heat.
6. Dip each piece of bread in the egg mixture coating both sides evenly.

7. Place stuffed bread slices in skillet and cook each side until golden brown.

8. Transfer the French toast to a baking sheet and bake in preheated oven for 15 minutes.

9. Serve almond-stuffed French toast topped with a sprinkle of powdered sugar and a drizzle of honey.

Nutrition Information:
Serving Size: 1 slice
Calories: 264
Fat: 13.3 g
Cholesterol: 79 mg
Sodium: 212 mg
Carbohydrates: 26.5 g
Protein: 8 g
Fiber: 2.7 g

88. Almond stuffed pork loin

Almond Stuffed Pork Loin is a flavorful and easy-to-make entree that makes for a perfect dinner for any occasion. The pork is stuffed with a savory mix of garlic, almonds, and herbs, then roasted to perfection. The end result is juicy, tender pork loin with a medley of flavors for your taste buds to enjoy!
Serving: 6
Preparation Time: 30 minutes
Ready Time: 1 hour

Ingredients:
- 2 lb pork loin
- 2 tablespoons olive oil
- 8 cloves garlic, finely chopped
- 2 tablespoons fresh thyme leaves
- 1/3 cup sliced almonds
- 2 tablespoons fresh rosemary leaves, chopped
- 1 teaspoon onion powder
- Salt and pepper to taste

Instructions:
1. Preheat the oven to 375 degrees Fahrenheit.
2. Rub the pork loin with olive oil and season with salt and pepper. Place on a cutting board and use a sharp knife to cut a pocket in the center, lengthwise, making sure to not go through the opposite side of the loin.
3. In a small bowl, mix together the garlic, thyme, almonds, rosemary, and onion powder.
4. Carefully stuff the pocket in the pork loin with the garlic and almond mixture.
5. Place on a baking sheet and roast for 45 minutes to an hour, or until the center is cooked through.
6. Slice and serve warm.

Nutrition Information:
Serving Size: 1 (115g)
Calories: 184 Calories
Total Fat: 8.8g
Cholesterol: 61mg
Sodium: 55mg
Total Carbohydrates: 2.3g
Protein: 24.8g

89. Almond-crusted salmon

Almond-crusted Salmon
This delicious and easy to execute dish is great for treating family or friends to a hearty meal. Salmon fillets are encrusted with a nutty crunch of almond meal and Parmesan, making sure the fish will be golden and crispy. Served with a light lemon-butter sauce, this special-occasion dish comes together in a snap.
Serving: 4
Preparation Time: 20 minutes
Ready Time: 35 minutes

Ingredients:
1/4 cup almond meal
3 tablespoons Parmesan cheese
Kosher salt and freshly ground black pepper

4 (6- to 8-ounce) salmon fillets, skin-on

2 tablespoons unsalted butter

2 cloves garlic, minced

3 tablespoons freshly squeezed lemon juice

2 tablespoons chopped fresh parsley

Instructions:

1. Preheat oven to 425°F.

2. In a small bowl, combine almond meal, Parmesan, 1/2 teaspoon each salt and pepper. Mix until well-combined.

3. Place salmon on a parchment-lined baking sheet. Sprinkle almond/Parmesan mixture evenly over each filet.

4. Bake for 15 minutes.

5. Meanwhile, in a small saucepan over medium heat, melt butter. Add garlic and cook for 30 seconds.

6. Add lemon juice and parsley, stirring to combine. Set aside.

7. Remove fish from oven. Pour butter mixture over top.

8. Continue baking for 5 minutes or until salmon is cooked through.

Nutrition Information:

Calories: 305, Fat: 20 g, Saturated fat: 5 g, Carbohydrates: 4 g, Protein: 29 g, Cholesterol: 80mg, Sodium: 238 mg

90. Almond-crusted scallops

Almond-crusted scallops are a delicious and easy seafood dish. This savory dish pairs sweet scallops with a crunchy almond crust that is sure to be a hit with every seafood lover.

Serving: 4

Preparation time: 15 minutes

Ready time: 15 minutes

Ingredients:

- 8 large scallops
- 1/2 cup blanched almonds
- 1 tablespoon olive oil
- Salt and pepper

Instructions:

1. Preheat the oven to 400°F
2. Spread the almonds on a baking sheet and toast for 3-4 minutes, stirring once after a couple minutes.
3. When the almonds are golden, remove them from the oven and let cool.
4. Place the scallops on a separate baking sheet.
5. Drizzle with the olive oil and season with salt and pepper.
6. Top the scallops with the toasted almonds.
7. Bake for 8-10 minutes, flipping the scallops halfway through.

Nutrition Information:

Calories: 202
Carbs: 5 grams
Protein: 20 grams
Fat: 11 grams

91. Almond chicken tenders

Almond Chicken Tenders
Serving: 4
Preparation time: 10 minutes
Ready time: 30 minutes

Ingredients:

- 2 cups almond flour
- 1 teaspoon garlic powder
- 1/4 teaspoon ground pepper
- 8 chicken tenders
- 2 eggs
- Cooking oil

Instructions:

1. In a shallow bowl, combine almond flour, garlic powder, and pepper.
2. In a separate bowl, beat the eggs.
3. Dip each chicken tender in the egg and then coat it with the almond flour mix.
4. Heat up a large skillet with cooking oil over medium-high heat.

5. Place the chicken tenders into the hot skillet and cook them for about 15 minutes, flipping them every 2 minutes.
6. Serve hot with a side of your favorite dipping sauce.

Nutrition Information:
Calories: 532
Total Fat: 27.6g
Saturated Fat: 3.4g
Cholesterol: 111mg
Sodium: 65mg
Carbohydrates: 21.5g
Fiber: 5.2g
Sugar: 8.8g
Protein: 55.7g

92. Almond-stuffed artichokes

Almond-Stuffed Artichokes
This delicious Italian-style dish is bursting with flavor, combining artichokes, garlic, and almonds. Satisfy your guests with these unique and easy-to-make stuffed artichokes.
Serving: 4
Preparation Time: 10 minutes
Ready Time: 45 minutes

Ingredients:
• 8 artichokes
• 1/2 cup almonds
• 1/4 teaspoon garlic powder
• 1/4 teaspoon dried oregano
• Salt and pepper to taste
• 2 tablespoons olive oil

Instructions:
1. Preheat oven to 350°F (177°C).
2. Cut off the artichoke stems and discard. Trim the artichoke leaves until they are all even. Cut artichokes in half and scoop out the inner parts to create a cavity.

3. Mix almonds, garlic powder, oregano, salt, and pepper in a bowl until well combined.
4. Fill each artichoke half with the almond mixture and drizzle with the olive oil.
5. Arrange artichokes on a baking sheet and bake in the oven for 45 minutes, or until artichokes are tender.

Nutrition Information:
Serving size: 1 artichoke half
Calories: 73
Total fat: 4.3g
Protein: 1.8g
Total Carbohydrate: 7.6g
Fiber: 4.1g

93. Almond salad dressing

This versatile Almond Salad Dressing is a delicious vegan and nut-free condiment that adds creamy richness to salads, steamed vegetables, and so much more.
Serving: Makes 1 cup of dressing.
Preparation Time: 10 minutes
Ready Time: 10 minutes

Ingredients:
• 1/3 cup freshly ground almonds
• 1/3 cup olive oil
• 1/2 cup filtered water
• 2 tablespoons freshly squeezed lemon juice
• 2 tablespoons white wine vinegar
• 2 cloves garlic, crushed
• 1 teaspoon Dijon mustard
• 1/2 teaspoon sea salt

Instructions:
1. Place all the Ingredients in a high-speed blender and blend until everything is well combined.

2. Pour the dressing into a jar with a lid and refrigerate until you use it. Shake before using.

Nutrition Information:
Calories: 204 | Fat: 20.3g | Saturated Fat: 2.8g | Sodium: 416mg | Carbohydrates: 3.3g | Fiber: 0.8g | Protein: 1.8g | Sugar: 0.6g

94. Almond butter frosting

Almond Butter Frosting
Serving: 12
Preparation Time: 10 minutes
Ready Time: 10 minutes

Ingredients:
- 3/4 cup almond butter
- 1/2 cup (1 stick) butter, softened
- 1/2 cup confectioners' sugar
- 1 teaspoon vanilla extract
- 1 pinch ground nutmeg (optional)

Instructions:
1. In a large bowl, combine almond butter, butter, confectioners' sugar, vanilla extract and nutmeg (if desired).
2. Using an electric mixer, beat Ingredients at low speed until smooth.
3. Increase mixer speed and continue to beat for an additional minute.
4. Serve frosting immediately, or cover and chill for up to 1 hour before using.

Nutrition Information (per serving):
Calories: 207 kcal, Carbohydrates: 7.8g, Protein: 3.2g, Fat: 17.3g, Saturated Fat: 5.6g, Cholesterol: 18.9mg, Sodium: 125.4mg, Fiber: 1.7g, Sugar: 5.4g
Sweet and creamy almond butter frosting is a delicious topping for cakes, cupcakes and other desserts. This delightful frosting requires just a few Ingredients and is ready in minutes – perfect for those in a hurry!

95. Almond cheesecake

Almond cheesecake is a delicious and creamy dessert that is perfect for the holidays or any special occasion. It combines the nutty sweetness of almond with the rich creaminess of cheesecake, creating the perfect balance of flavors. This recipe will show you how to make an almond cheesecake that everyone will love.

Serving: 8-10
Preparation Time: 30 minutes
Ready Time: 6 hours 30 minutes

Ingredients:
- 3/4 cup graham cracker crumbs
- 3 tablespoons granulated sugar
- 3 tablespoons butter, melted
- 2 packages (8 ounces each) cream cheese, softened
- 1 can (14 ounces) sweetened condensed milk
- 2 eggs
- 2 tablespoons almond extract
- 1 cup sliced almonds

Instructions:
1. Preheat oven to 350°F. Grease 9-inch springform pan.
2. In small bowl, combine cracker crumbs, sugar and butter. Press crumb mixture onto bottom and 1 inch up sides of prepared pan. Bake 10 minutes.
3. Meanwhile, in large bowl with mixer at medium speed, beat cream cheese until fluffy. At low speed, beat in sweetened condensed milk until blended. Beat in eggs and almond extract just until blended.
4. Pour cream cheese mixture over crust. Sprinkle with almonds.
5. Bake 25 to 30 minutes or until center is almost set. Turn off oven; let cheesecake stand in oven 1 hour.
6. Remove cheesecake from oven. Run knife around edge of pan to loosen cake; cool before removing side of pan.

Nutrition Information: Per Serving: Calories 426, Total Fat 24g, Saturated Fat 12g, Cholesterol 79mg, Sodium 277mg, Carbohydrates 45g, Dietary Fiber 1g, Protein 8g.

96. Almond fruit dip

Almond Fruit Dip
Serving: Makes about 1 cup of dip
Preparation Time: 10 minutes
Ready Time: 10 minutes

Ingredients:
- 2 tablespoons honey
- 1/3 cup almond butter
- 2 tablespoons freshly squeezed lemon juice
- 1/4 teaspoon cinnamon
- Pinch of nutmeg

Instructions:
1. In a small bowl, combine the honey, almond butter, lemon juice, cinnamon, and nutmeg.
2. Mix until Ingredients are fully-combined and a creamy texture is reached.
3. Serve dip with sliced fruits.

Nutrition Information: Each 2 tablespoons of this almond fruit dip contains approximately 130 calories, 8 grams of fat, 9 grams of carbohydrates, and 3.5 grams of protein.

97. Almond-flavored whipped cream

This simple yet delicious almond-flavored cream makes an excellent topping or filling for cakes, pies, doughnuts, and more.
Serving: Serves 8
Preparation time: 5 minutes
Ready time: 5 minutes

Ingredients:
- 2 cups heavy whipping cream
- ½ cup powdered sugar
- 1 teaspoon almond extract

Instructions:
1. In a large bowl, whip cream until soft peaks form.
2. Add in powdered sugar and almond extract and continue to whip until stiff peaks form.
3. Serve immediately or store in the refrigerator for up to 1 day.

Nutrition Information (per serving): Calories: 168; Total fat: 15g; Saturated fat: 9g; Cholesterol: 51mg; Sodium: 16mg; Carbohydrates: 9g; Protein: 1g.

98. Almond custard

Almond Custard - This classic, creamy custard is made with just a few simple Ingredients and is perfect for dessert or breakfast.
Serving: 4
Preparation Time: 10 minutes
Ready Time: 40 minutes

Ingredients:
- 2 cups evaporated milk
- 1/2 cup sugar
- 4 egg yolks
- 1 teaspoon almond extract
- 1/4 teaspoon salt

Instructions:
1. Preheat oven to 350 degrees F.
2. Combine the evaporated milk, sugar, egg yolks, almond extract and salt in a bowl and whisk until smooth.
3. Pour the mixture into an 8x8 inch baking dish.
4. Bake for 30-35 minutes until the custard is set.
5. Let cool before serving.

Nutrition Information:
Calories: 194 kcal
Carbohydrates: 17 g
Protein: 5 g
Fat: 12 g

Saturated Fat: 4 g
Cholesterol: 100 mg
Sodium: 174 mg
Potassium: 145 mg
Sugar: 14 g
Vitamin A: 308 IU
Calcium: 129 mg

99. Almond pie

Almond Pie is an incredibly delicious dessert with a crunchy almond crust and creamy almond filling. The perfect way to enjoy sweet almonds!
Serving: 8-10
Preparation Time: 15 minutes
Ready Time: 1 hour

Ingredients:
- 2 cups all-purpose flour
- 1 teaspoon salt
- 1 cup butter, cold
- 2 tablespoons cider vinegar
- ¼ cup cold water
- 3/4 cup sugar
- 2 teaspoons almond extract
- 2 eggs
- 1/2 cup toasted slivered almonds

Instructions:
1. Preheat oven to 375 degrees F.
2. In a large bowl, combine flour, salt, butter, and vinegar. Mix with your fingertips until it resembles crumbs.
3. Add cold water to the mixture. Stir until it forms a dough.
4. Roll out the dough and press into a 9-inch pie pan.
5. In a separate bowl, combine sugar, almond extract, eggs, and almonds. Mix until blended.
6. Pour mixture into the prepared crust.
7. Bake for 45 minutes or until golden brown.

Nutrition Information:
Serving Size: 1 Slice
Calories: 400
Fat: 20g
Carbohydrates: 44g
Protein: 6g
Sugars: 23g
Sodium: 300mg

100. Almond milk hot cereal

Almond Milk Hot Cereal: This nutty cereal made with creamy almond milk is a delicious and healthy breakfast option that is sure to please.
Serving: 4
Preparation Time: 5 minutes
Ready Time: 10 minutes

Ingredients:
2 cups almond milk
1/2 cup rolled oats
1/2 teaspoon ground cinnamon
1 teaspoon pure vanilla extract
1 tablespoon brown sugar
1/2 cup dried fruits

Instructions:
1. In a medium saucepan, heat almond milk over medium heat.
2. Once the almond milk is hot, add the oats, cinnamon, vanilla extract, and brown sugar and stir to combine.
3. Cook over medium heat for about 5 minutes, stirring occasionally, until oats are cooked.
4. Remove from heat and stir in dried fruits.
5. Serve hot.

Nutrition Information:
Per Serving:

Calories: 145 kcal, Carbohydrates: 23 g, Protein: 4 g, Fat: 4 g, Saturated Fat: 0 g, Cholesterol: 0 mg, Sodium: 24 mg, Potassium: 131 mg, Fiber: 2 g, Sugar: 11 g, Vitamin A: 33 IU, Vitamin C: 0 mg, Calcium: 161 mg, Iron: 0 mg

101. Almond banana pancakes

These almond banana pancakes are a delicious and healthy breakfast entrée that is sure to satisfy your sweet tooth.
Serving: Makes 6-7 pancakes
Preparation Time: 5 minutes
Ready Time: 15 minutes

Ingredients:
- 1 cup all-purpose flour
- 2 teaspoons baking powder
- 1/4 teaspoon salt
- 2 mashed ripe bananas
- 2 tablespoons honey
- 1 cup almond milk
- 2 tablespoons melted butter
- 1/4 cup slivered almonds

Instructions:
1. In a medium bowl, whisk together the flour, baking powder and salt.
2. In a separate bowl, mix together the mashed bananas, honey, almond milk and melted butter.
3. Pour the wet Ingredients into the dry Ingredients and mix until just combined.
4. Heat a greased skillet over medium heat and add the batter in batches, about ¼ cup at a time.
5. Cook until bubbles appear on the top and the bottom is lightly browned. Flip and continue to cook for about 2 minutes.
6. Transfer pancakes to a plate and top with slivered almonds.

Nutrition Information:

Calories: 286, Total Fat: 10 g, Saturated Fat: 5 g, Trans Fat: 0 g, Cholesterol: 15 mg, Sodium: 225 mg, Potassium: 372 mg, Total Carbohydrates: 41 g, Dietary Fiber: 3 g, Sugars: 11 g, Protein: 7 g.

102. Almond roasted turkey

Almond Roasted Turkey
Serving: 4 people
Preparation Time: 10 mins.
Ready Time: 1 hour

Ingredients:
- 2 pound turkey
- 2 tablespoons olive oil
- 1 tsp garlic powder
- 1 tsp italian seasoning
- ½ tsp salt
- 1 tbsp raw almonds, finely chopped
- 2 ounces of butter, melted

Instructions:
1. Preheat oven to 350 degrees F.
2. Place turkey in a baking pan and rub with olive oil.
3. Sprinkle garlic powder, Italian seasoning, and salt over turkey.
4. Sprinkle chopped almonds on turkey.
5. Bake for 30 minutes.
6. Increase heat to 425 degrees F and bake for an additional 30 minutes.
7. Baste turkey with melted butter and bake for an additional 10 minutes or until golden brown and cooked through.

Nutrition Information:
Calories: 238; Fat: 10.7 g; Protein: 15.3 g; Carbohydrates: 4.3 g; Fiber: 0.9 g; Sugar: 0.4 g; Sodium: 447 mg.

103. Almond breaded shrimp

Almond Breaded Shrimp

Serving: 4
Preparation Time: 15 minutes
Ready Time: 40 minutes

Ingredients:
- 1 pound large shrimp, peeled and deveined
- 2 eggs
- 2 tablespoons cold water
- 1 cup all-purpose flour
- 1 teaspoon baking powder
- 1 teaspoon garlic powder
- 1 teaspoon mustard powder
- 1 teaspoon salt
- 2 cup finely chopped, slivered almonds
- Vegetable oil, such as canola oil, for frying

Instructions:
1. Begin by preparing the shrimp; peel and devein the shrimp, then let them sit in a colander while you prepare the almond coating.
2. In a shallow bowl, whisk together the eggs and cold water. Combine the flour, baking powder, garlic powder, mustard powder, and salt in a separate bowl.
3. Rinse the shrimp in cool water and pat dry with a paper towel.
4. To coat the shrimp, dip each shrimp into the egg mixture and then into the flour mixture, making sure they are completely coated.
5. Dip the shrimp back into the egg mixture, then the almond coating.
6. Heat the vegetable oil in a large skillet over medium heat. The oil should be at least 1-2 inches deep in the skillet.
7. Fry the shrimp in the oil about 2 minutes per side, until golden brown. Using a slotted spoon or spatula, remove the shrimp to a plate lined with paper towels to drain.

Nutrition Information:
Calories: 468, Total Fat: 28g, Cholesterol: 314mg, Sodium: 984mg, Total Carbohydrates: 25g, Dietary Fiber: 3g, Sugars: 2g, Protein: 30g

CONCLUSION

In conclusion, Almond Delights: 103 Delectable Recipes is a must-have cookbook for anyone who loves almonds and wants to explore new ways to incorporate them into their meals and snacks. The author, Rose Hunter, has put together an excellent collection of recipes that range from sweet to savory, simple to complex, and healthy to indulgent. From almond-crusted chicken to almond butter fudge brownies, the possibilities are endless.

One of the standout aspects of this cookbook is the variety of recipes. Whether you're a novice or an experienced cook, there's something for everyone. The recipes are easy to follow, and the ingredients are readily available at most grocery stores. What's more, the cookbook is beautifully designed, with stunning photos that make the recipes come to life.

Another strength of Almond Delights is that the recipes are adaptable. If you're looking for a gluten-free or vegan option, for example, there are plenty of options. You can also customize the recipes to suit your personal preferences. For example, if you prefer your cookies less sweet, you can reduce the amount of sugar.

Something else that sets this cookbook apart is the health benefits of almonds. Almonds are packed with nutrients that are good for you, including protein, fiber, and healthy fats. They're also low in carbs, making them a great addition to a variety of diets. By incorporating more almonds into your meals and snacks, you can improve your overall health and well-being.

Overall, Almond Delights: 103 Delectable Recipes is a well-written, well-researched cookbook that deserves a spot in every kitchen. It's perfect for anyone who loves almonds and wants to explore new ways to use this versatile ingredient. Whether you're looking for a new breakfast idea or a dessert to impress your guests, this cookbook has you covered. So go ahead and give it a try – you won't be disappointed!

Printed in Great Britain
by Amazon

26762531R00059